CRANBROOK VOICES FROM THE 20th CENTURY

A collection of recorded memories highlighting facets of life in Cranbrook during the last hundred years.

Published by the Cranbrook and District Local History Society, December 2000.
Registered charity number : 265889

Printed by Rother Valley Press Ltd, Tenterden, Kent.

All rights reserved. No part of this publication may be reproduced, stored in a retrieval system, or transmitted, in any form or by any means electronic, mechanical, photocopying, recording or otherwise without the permission of the Cranbrook and District Local History Society.

ISBN 0-9539667-0-4

© 2000 Cranbrook and District Local History Society.

CONTENTS

4 Foreword
6 Introduction

8 Everybody knew everybody
10 Places
15 Quiet?
19 Agriculture
27 Farm Workers
30 Hop Picking
34 The Poor
38 Road and Rail
44 Amusements and Entertainments
53 World War Two
57 Church & Chapel
65 Primary Schools
72 Secondary Schools
80 Medicine
85 Shops
95 The Hand Laundry
100 Some 'Characters'
104 Bill Jempson

110 Index of contributors

FOREWORD

This collection of memories - or should I call it an anthology? - is an invaluable record of life in Cranbrook in the last hundred years, and a fascinating portrait of individuals who lived and worked in the town. They come from all walks of life. Their recollections are vivid and their language, thank goodness, has not been polished by the editors. It is an authentic record of change such as occurred in every English town, but in a market town like Cranbrook change was particularly rapid, keeping pace with the revolution in agriculture since the Second World War.

I first came to know Cranbrook in 1930, when my parents bought Sissinghurst Castle and began to make their famous garden there. On our very first visit we called at the shop in Stone Street run by Charles Evernden, who produced from his inexhaustible store a print of the Castle from Hasted's History of Kent, and it was this that determined my mother to buy it. Since then Cranbrook has been our shopping town, and the centre of many activities in which I am glad to have played a small part.

But reading this book, I now realise how little I knew of our neighbours' lives. The earliest interviews preserve memories of much misery and injustice, when farm labourers worked and lived in abominable conditions, their children ill-fed, their cottages in disrepair, and when they grew too old to work, they were evicted from them with the workhouse or their children's cottages as their only refuge.

Then conditions slowly improved. Derelict housing was replaced, schools multiplied, public transport was better organised, nutrition and public hygiene were immeasurably advanced. Cranbrook gained a cinema, for a time a theatre, playing fields, supermarkets, but still the shape of the place remained the same, based upon the classic triangle of all small towns - the church, the inn, and the school. People were no less industrious and, I venture to say, happier, as their horizons expanded.

So in a way this book is a celebration of mounting prosperity and continuing success. With its abundant illustrations it shows how our town has shaken off the worst of the past and kept the best. Its High Street is a panorama of changing English architecture. The book is an equally honest record of triumphs and mistakes. These memories could have been preserved in no other way than by recorded interviews. Few of these people, one of whom was born as early as 1887, would have troubled to set them down in writing, thinking them unimportant. But having this book before us, we know that they are of supreme importance, and a significant contribution to the social history of England as a whole.

Nigel Nicolson
President
Cranbrook and District Local History Society

INTRODUCTION

For its contribution to the millennium celebrations, Cranbrook Local History Society has chosen to concentrate on oral history, and to produce a volume based on interviews with inhabitants of the town, recalling memories of the past hundred years.

Oral history has many advantages. It is fun to do, and amateurs can feel they are making a genuine contribution to historical knowledge. There is a sense of urgency about it - material not recorded now may be lost for ever - and the spoken word has a vividness and immediacy which eludes other methods of research.

Unfortunately we have not been able to interview everybody whose contribution might have been useful, so the editors would like to apologise to anyone who might feel excluded, while thanking all those who agreed to submit to ordeal by cassette recorder. Thanks and apologies also go to volunteers whose contributions we were unable to use.

The recollections contained here are personal; memories may have failed from time to time and opinions are subjective. We have made no attempt to impose an official editorial line on the contents, and we have kept editorial comment to a minimum, preferring to let the voices of the century speak for themselves.

People returning to Cranbrook after an absence of several years often comment that it is like walking into the past, so little has changed. Although it may be the town is at times a little slow to adapt to new ideas, we believe that this volume will show that impression to be largely illusory. Those with longer memories are more inclined to emphasise the ways in which the twentieth century was a period of rapid evolution in the life of Cranbrook.

A group of members of the society started work early in 1999. We were fortunate to find extremely valuable material already existing in the form of interviews on tape, including those made by Charles Forward, Sidney Barham and Charles Evernden as long ago as the 1970s. These not only provided us with some of the most interesting observations, but also enabled us to reach back to before the First World War.

Over a period of eighteen months, the group recorded interviews with some thirty Cranbrookians, to add to the tapes we already had. In selecting passages for inclusion, the editors have tried to maintain a balance between the important elements in the life of the community, and to include a mixture of anecdote and nostalgia on the one hand, and more reflective comment on the other. We hope that the book will appeal both to local people and to those with a broader interest in the social history of the twentieth century.

The society would like to thank Dr John Whyman, formerly of the University of Kent, who pioneered oral history in the county and who gave us much valuable guidance on interview techniques and the compilation of an historical record based on the spoken word. We are also grateful to Dr Michael Winstanley for making available the transcripts of interviews with Sidney Barham and Charles Evernden. Photographs are taken from the society's own archives or from the private collections of members.

The book was produced with the aid of a grant from the Kent History Fund, to whom we would like to express our thanks and gratitude.

EVERYBODY KNEW EVERYBODY

Nick Metson, *born in Cranbrook, 1918.*

By the 1940s, I wasn't *au fait* with all the people like we used to be. Originally you knew everybody, and who married who, because everybody married the girls of the town. You knew who they were and who their fathers were.

Charles Forward, *born locally in 1906, retained memories of Cranbrook and Sissinghurst before 1914, which he recorded in the 1970s.*

A few of the middle class might have had a horse, but apart from that people got about on foot or bicycle. And as a consequence people didn't move around like they do now. And there were huge clans, almost, of people in this district all the same name. A huge number of Gurrs, Wellers, Smiths and Taylors. And you used to distinguish between them: "Which Taylor is this? Oh, charcoal burners." You'd sort of distinguish them: Pigsfoot Taylor or Charcoal Taylor or Smith the Glover and Fiddler Smith and all such names as that, and as soon as you said that they knew which Taylor you were talking about.

There were enough Wellers here that they formed a glee club, and there was enough Gurrs that they formed a brass band - but that was just dying out when I can remember. I can't remember the band but I know some of the Gurrs that was in the band.

My father told me a story once that happened on Cranbrook Common right on the junction where the Maidstone road and the Sissinghurst road goes down. He was working in a garden there and one of the Wellers met one of the Gurrs. They was both keen singers and right in the middle of that junction they challenged one another to a duet and they stood and sang in the middle of the road. And my father was in the hedge and he said, "I moved up the hedge", he said, "and I tell you my boy it was worth listening to."

Rodney Dann, *born in Cranbrook, 1940.*

When I was at school, everybody knew everybody. People are more remote with each other now, and of course the volume of housing...

Pat Duxbury (nee **Cash**), *born in Cranbrook, 1935.*

It was a very close community. I came from Court Stile. It hadn't got the council houses then: there were old houses there, now some eight of them pulled down. Everybody helped each other, everybody knew each other - they fell out as well, but they shared. Now these little communities have got swallowed up into a big area. Families had always been there - we all knew back to grandad. You shared the children out - if mum went out to work, fruit picking, a neighbour took charge of the children. When you came home from school you reported to her. There wasn't the transport of course, so you stayed close. The war made a big difference - the evacuees- for years, people resented the ones that stayed - they were intruders. Some have stayed on and are still here, have intermarried and become part of the community. But initially that was an intrusion.

PLACES

Although Cranbrook seems to be much the same as it was fifty or a hundred years ago, a great deal of development has taken place, and some old landmarks have disappeared.

Garry Blanch *went to look at some places he remembers .*

I went to look at the new buildings they are erecting behind Gough's *(Shepherds, High Street)*, and I walked up through the piece of land I owned ... And I was looking there and I saw the old sluice gates which must have been part of the old watercress beds. These watercress beds stretched right up along the back and up virtually where the council offices are; they grew watercress as a commercial venture and the spring, well, it must be a spring of clear water which the watercress grew in... These would have been rectangular beds which would have been tended and the watercress would have been harvested and sold to local shops.

The Horse Pond, I can remember, there was a fence across the middle. The fenced area used to belong to Bill Cooper, who owned the Moat, but the rest of it appeared to be public. When we were kids we used to go fishing for newts, and then you put them back... There used to be hundreds of them in there.

And old Bart, a very old man who used to have a field up where the new primary school is. At about four o'clock in the afternoon he would bring all his cows down and they would get their water from the Horse Pond. I don't know how it came to be enclosed because it was a public watering area for the horses, which would have been the pack horses, well, in medieval times when the wool trade was in full swing in Cranbrook. Where the car parks are either side of the church boiler house, there were stables for these horses. Also if you go along by the fish shop in the High Street, it's called Horse Entry, a lot of these pack horses used to go through there.

Ted Ratcliff *deplores the demolition of the Bull Hotel.*

That's when they committed murder - the Bull Hotel - they demolished that, in 1936 that was pulled down. Winch and Son were brewers and they were down at Baker's Cross. Winches were auctioneers and estate agents, and they also had farms. Frank Winch had a farm over at Brick Kiln, just over there. They were brewers and they owned the Bull Hotel, which was a pub actually, not a hotel. Leslie Green came along and wanted to extend his business, and they just let him pull the Bull down - just like that. A wicked shame, terrible, because it was a beautiful old building - weather-boarded.

Edward Ryan *remembers some of the cottages that have been demolished.*

There was a row of houses in the Tanyard. There's a building there now which belongs to old Joe Brown's shop which had previously been the stables to the pub *(now Swan Antiques)*, the Prince Albert pub. But that closed in 1915, they tell me. All those buildings there which are now made into small houses, it continued on there, and it was all cottages there, quite a few cottages, and also more over the other side. But with all these cottages, the people only paid five shillings a week rent.

After the war we had a Labour government which said there had got to be houses fit for heroes to live in. There were whole rows of houses, like down Bank Street - there were thirteen houses, changed hands for £300 a time. But the houses that did escape it were houses in Crane Lane... Now those cottages, which were sold in 1955 for £500, the last time one came up for sale it was £74,000.

Places

Some houses were demolished because they fell apart, but that was the people who lived in them, that was really their fault. Houses are only what people are that live in them. The landlord could do nothing. After the war, with a Labour government, the Council had so much power. There was Mr XX on the Council, he was drunk with power, telling you what you had to do with your houses, it was impossible to carry on... All around were demolished in the madness of the '50s. There had got to be no slums in Cranbrook. There were slums, like Bank Street was. If they'd looked after the houses and kept them, they'd have been there now. Rangers Row pulled down; there was Bank Street; West End Terrace. You'd never know there had been a row of houses up there - opposite the Duke of York pub. All this lot in the Tanyard; Crown Court came down. The house we lived in, No 1 Crown Court, it should never have been pulled down. Beautiful beamed place, and everything else.

Doris Dapson *lived just off the High Street.*

I lived in 9 Shepherd's Cottages, in Causton Road, just off the High Street, so really right in the town. Behind there was just fields, there was no houses. There wasn't much in the fields behind, it was all farm land in those days. And the field behind was owned by an old man called Bartholomew. We always called it Bart's Field. And it's Bart's Field to this day although it's built on - Hendley Drive now.

Where the post office, the sorting office is, when I was a child there was an old inn called the Crane Inn on the front and behind them was all these little cottages. The row of cottages was condemned but they are still lived in today... And of course, Lloyds bank isn't an old building, only the chimney. That's been completely rebuilt, because that was Miss Wood's house. Dr Wood was her father and she died just before the war.

Places

The allotments were much bigger. They came right the way down where they've built houses... The road went up still where it does now, but it was a little old road. Rope Walk, that was a path; well you couldn't get through there, only to the farm. It was just Bank Street, which I think was originally called Brewhouse Lane because I understand from my father that there was a brewery down there once, and there must have been slaughterhouses as well because I've seen a picture of my father standing in front of a slaughterhouse and he told me it was Bank Street.

The Bottoms was a farm... where, as you go down from Crane Lane and up the path, where you hit the bottom of the brookside, that was called Bottoms. And there was a farm there, and I think Mr Jempson owned it and there was an apple orchard all round there. And the road still went up which was called Freight Lane, up to the farm. But they enlarged Frythe Way at the end of the war, because German prisoners worked on that first bit... I remember seeing them when I walked with my mother, working in the road.

Peter Jempson *has recollections of Back Lane (now Angley Road).*

You had to be careful on your bike when Jack Brown was driving his cows across from what is now the Angley School site to be milked, because it got very slippery as he would drive them rather fast. You were OK if two cars wanted to pass in those days, but if you met a hop-pocket lorry, you had to take evasive action. We moved to another old building on the other side of the Crane Valley, called Bottoms Farm, which had about four acres of land which my father had as a smallholding...It was a very ancient rather ramshackle old cottage, next door to where the Scout Hut is now.

*Above : Sheep grazing where the clinic now stands
Below : Rectory Farm by the Horse Pond,
now the Museum.*

14

QUIET?

Charles Forward.

I was born in 1906. I suppose the most noticeable thing in those days was the quietness. No cars or machinery. There was no mechanisation on the farm whatever - no tractors, no combine harvesters, fruit washers. There was nothing of that. No power source polluting. There was hardly any traffic on the roads at all in the way of motors and sometimes you might not see a motor in a day. There was no aeroplanes overhead because in those days navigation was in its infancy and they navigated mostly by landmarks. An evident landmark in this district was the railway line running from Cranbrook to London and the coast via Tonbridge and Ashford, you see. And in the distance sometimes in those days, a rare occasion, if you could hear the hum of an aeroplane everybody would rush out: "Aeroplane! Aeroplane!" We'd just see a black spot in the distance going 'down the line' or 'up the line', we used to say, as the case might be.

Brian Brew, *born in Cranbrook, 1930.*

One thing I can remember is the quietness and lack of transport on the roads. Particularly the farm children used to have seasonal games on the road - tops at one time, football and cricket. This of course was the Glassenbury to Hartley road. Occasionally they had to stop, maybe for a Brooke Bond tea van or some sort of small type of car which went at about twenty miles an hour. They'd get off the road for that, then they'd go back again and maybe half an hour later there'd be something else - you'd hear a traction engine from Hartley.

Quiet ?

But not so quiet in the centre of Cranbrook. **'Sonny' Hall,** *Biddenden farmer, born around 1908, recalled the 1920s.*

At the Mill, there was a lot of coming and going - a place to get fodder for cattle and sheep, small quantities of flour and stuff, I think. The Mill in those days ran all day and every day, in order to keep it going whether there was a wind or not. There was a big gas engine - you'd hear it all over the town. It ran all day - toop, toop - doing only about two hundred revs a minute.

Brigid Longley, *born in Cranbrook, 1925.*

To give you some idea of the amount of traffic, when I was about seven, I suppose, I was allowed to go out on the road on my bicycle. And I used to go and visit a friend in Benenden, but on condition that I got off each time a car came. And occasionally I got to Benenden and back and I hadn't got off once. So things were very different.

But Cranbrook itself was always a bustling place. When you think of the animals being driven up Stone Street and High Street to go to the two slaughterhouses behind the two butchers' shops, there was a lot of noise. And the blacksmith you could hear all up Stone Street: you could hear the lovely clink of him working. Lots of horses delivering things and a great deal of bustle. And then in hop picking time utter chaos, with hundreds of people coming into town at the weekends, and in the evenings getting drunk, and quite a bit of violence even in those days. It wasn't any quieter in many ways at all.

Charles Evernden *recalled one traditional way of reducing the street noise.*

Used to be a custom, you know, if anyone was seriously ill in the town anywhere, they used to put straw down in the roads to deaden the noise of the traffic... It used to be half covered with straw to deaden the noise of the horses and wagons. I don't know whether it saved anybody's life or not, but that was the idea... When I was a boy it was always done... it was done up to between the wars.

If this failed to save a life, the passing bell was tolled. **Sidney Barham** *recalled his childhood memories at the very beginning of the century.*

Anybody who was really fit to die, as it were, had to have a passing bell: it wasn't really right if you didn't... Then of course everybody would know there was somebody dead, you see. Now who's dead, who's that? It brought the thing home to you far more than it does now... And of course people in the know could tell the age and sex, I think, of the person, by the way in which the bell rang. Well, I never knew that. But I know it used to start off with a very heavy boom, like that. Then there'd be a long... then another boom. It would go several times like that. Then it would start to get louder and louder, and quicker and quicker and quicker, until it became almost a wail. Then it would stop. Then of course: "Who's dead?" - the question would go round.

Above : Wilsley Pound, now a roundabout.

Below : Waterloo Road, with the Police Station on the right, where the Queen's Hall now stands.

AGRICULTURE

Bill King, *born in 1929, has lived in Cranbrook since the age of three.*

I left school in 1943 at fourteen and worked at Hocken's at Little Glassenbury. There was seventeen in the place, I think - there's one that does the work now. I did a six day week, ten hour a day, sixty hour for the grand sum of thirty shillings a week.

The change in dairy farming! There's nothing left in Cranbrook - to what it was then! You could start off in Bank Street in Cranbrook, there was a farmer there by name of Bartholomew. He milked cows: he used to drive them up Bank Street through the town, and they used to graze on Ball Field while we was at school. And then you come up the road a bit further to Causton Road and there was a chap there named Mr Smith - he used to deliver milk on a barrow with his churn. We went a few hundred yards up the road and there was Mr Webb. He milked cows - he used to go round Goudhurst with his milk. You remember he used to come through with an old Austin brown car?

Go up as far as the War Memorial, turn back along New Road a little way and there was Jack Brown. He milked cows. Goddards Green Farm, that was the Enfields' - they milked cows there. We go up a bit, just turn up Huggins Hall Lane and there was Jack Rolfe: he'd just got started, I think it was about the '60s, he had foot and mouth and cleared him right out. So he never milked there no more.

Down to Swattenden School: Jack White, he milked cows - he's gone. Come back up the top to Gate Farm - Frank

Agriculture

Chapman, he milked cows. You could go round and buy your milk from the dairy. Come back up to Hartley again - there was George Rogers: you could buy milk there round the back. John Wickham was the last one round there milking.

At Hocken's, there was one of the biggest dairy farms. At Glassenbury and Little Glassenbury. They done a milk round. When I was there they had two milk floats on the road, two ponies and traps and an electric. And they were the first ones who brought the third of a pint bottles to the schools.

Come down to Park Farm. Stan Morris was there - he milked cows. Then John Coombe-Jones took it, and that's finished now....

Brigid Longley *used to milk Queen Marie of Yugoslavia's herd of Jersey cows at Buckhurst Farm in the late 1940s.*

I was using a milking machine by then to milk the cows - a small herd. And looking after them completely. As the herd was only getting going, we had under twenty. I think we had only about sixteen we were milking. Nowadays it would be a ridiculous number but in those days it was probably quite an average number for a small herd. The milk we separated some and I actually made butter for the Royal slice of bread - but most of the milk went to the Milk Marketing Board. It was picked up with a milk lorry - this was before tanks. And it went into churns and we cooled the milk over an old fashioned cooler where the milk runs down the outside and the cold water was on the inside. Not very efficient, but adequate - into churns, and then the lorry picked up the churns.

I was up very early and started milking about half past six. To start with I was on a bicycle, and then I had an old Austin Ten. Then to save petrol I would come back on my bicycle for lunch

Agriculture

and then go back on the bike and come home in the evening in the car.

Major Enfield's *father owned Goddards Green Farm (40 acres) and Brick Kiln Farm (98 acres). The family moved here from Sutton Valence in the 1930s.*

We had some farms in Cranbrook, some in Sutton Valence, and the journey in those days from one to the other, if you've only got a horse and cart, it took rather a long time. And it was all done on account of hop quotas. If you grew hops you had to have a quota and the quota went with the farms, but there were ways and means of taking the quota from one farm to the other. So we brought the quota from Sutton Valence to Cranbrook because Sutton Valence was the old type of hop fields: they were done, grown up poles, thin chestnut poles fourteen foot long, and the farm at Cranbrook had wirework on, so that was a permanent fixture, where you could string them easy with a stringing pole and a coil of string.

(In addition to hop fields and dairy,) we used to grow corn, peas, broad beans, funnily enough. They were very dusty things to harvest, I must say. We grew peas, we had oats and barley and wheat, but this was all done by hand, everything was worked in by hand, even sown by a fiddle. You carry, what shall I say, about 28 pound of corn in it. And you worked it like playing a fiddle or a violin. It's like this, you put your left foot forward, push your bow to the left, put your right foot forward, pull your bow back to the right.

That changed I suppose just before the war, I should imagine. Then we started getting tractors which they were, I must say, the early tractors were iron wheels: there was no such thing as rubber tyres on tractors and everything was pulled by a tractor.

Agriculture

John Wickham *has been farming since 1952, after three years training at Sissinghurst Castle Farm. He was asked first about the 1950s and 1960s.*

There were quite a lot more farms in Cranbrook than today. I've been trying to work the number out and I think it was 26. On average, a fair bit smaller than today - our two farms were 200 acres and 150 acres. There were two large estates: Glassenbury (the Roberts family) and the Bedgebury crown estates. For the most part I'd say the pattern was of ownership, not renting.

Hops and dairying were the main two activities - lots of farms would do both. But there was other farming done - mostly fruit growing and some arable. Farming was the most important source of local livelihood. Every farm employed a number of workers, and their wives generally did farm work too, though we did take on occasional workers - including the Londoners for hop picking and casual gipsy labour - at the busy times. But both hops and dairying were quite heavily labour intensive: for the hops there was a lot to be done on the wirework over the winter.

He compared this with farming in the last quarter of the century, since Britain's joining the Common Market.

The acreage of hop growing is much lower, of course - there's only one hop grower in Cranbrook now. At first it was the verticilium wilt that caused quite a few people to get out of hops in the 1960s. Farmers round here grew Fuggles hops and they were particularly hit, though some switched to wilt-tolerant varieties of hops.

Above : 1906 postcard of London hop-pickers on their way to the station.

Below : Harvesting at Cranbrook, early 1900s.

Agriculture

Much less dairying too. In fact there's not a dairy farm left in Cranbrook - only Reynolds at Benenden and Mr Smith at Goudhurst. But there's been more fruit growing - soft fruit, though Stanley Calcutt always grew currants back in the early days... *(To a question about apples.)* The most obvious change is from big trees to bush trees...We only used to grow culinary apples - Bramleys and Derbies - but now there are many more dessert apples being grown, with more varieties... Our growers found European competition difficult, especially Golden Delicious, but now we've established our own dessert apples...

We used to sell mainly to the London wholesalers, but the supermarkets have changed things enormously. Nowadays we have to form co-ops to supply them: in fact, European grants only go to co-ops. And the quality of products has to be very high to satisfy the supermarkets...

'Set aside' came in 1989. We had to record what was grown in each field, and still have to. Then we are paid for a percentage of the arable fields not planted - 10% at present...

Farmers can survive. But they must be able to adapt. I've changed from being a dairy and hop farmer to a fruit farmer. And farms are going to have to diversify more - including bed and breakfast and other activities of that sort.

Bill Calcutt *took over farming at Four Wents from his uncle Stanley in 1982. He commented on the limited change to field shapes over the second half of the century.*

When I took over in 1982, I went through all the field areas and all of the little bits of woodland, shaws and things, to see how much productive farmland there was out of the 150 acres, and then to see what I could do to improve it. I actually only took out half an acre of scrubby old thing that was full of rabbits and bullfinches, and everything else I've left alone. Because on a farm like this you need to have shaws and hedges and tall hedges - lewing. We've got pole lewing, we've got ordinary old-fashioned traditional type of lewing down on the Glassenbury Road. It'll raise temperature by several degrees in an orchard when you're trying to get pollinating. It doesn't blow your hop heads off - and all sorts of pluses. So I think the field shapes are very much the same as they would have been in grandfather's time.

Over the years hops have been grubbed and currants planted, and currants grubbed and apples planted - and so we go round in circles, trying to keep ahead of the job if we can. But we're still about a third hops, a third top fruit and a third soft fruit which now is all blackcurrants. The redcurrants as well as the blueberries have come to an end which is a great pity, but if you can't sell something profitably they have to come out.

He was asked about the Common Market's impact.

I don't think really that the Common Market has had very much to do with what we do, because we've always been exposed to competition. There's no sort of subsidy on top fruit growing, nor on soft fruit growing. It's really a matter of where the apples come from and where other soft fruit comes from... Certainly when the Hops Marketing Board came to an end we entered into a very different style of selling hops. We were told that we had to have forward contracts and no longer have quota, basic quota and annual quota, as in the past. And the brewers took advantage of this in that they were able to import hops from America, Germany or anywhere else they wished to. And I think that general trends are that more and more people prefer to drink lager which generally speaking isn't made with seeded hops which traditionally we've always grown.

Agriculture

He was asked whether most farmers were now in Growers Associations, or whether many independent growers survived.

John Breach will tell you about the British Independent Fruit Growers Association, and I guess there's quite a few of them. But uncle Stanley was a very early member of the Apple Growers Association at Horsmonden - that's one of the very earliest apple co-operatives in the country to be still operating. I'm presently chairman of that. We mainly do storage now, because a couple of years back we formed a new joint venture company called Anderida Packers with SGT, the Society of Growers of Top Fruit, who are our marketing arm... One thing where we are getting help from Brussels is that we have a thing called an operating fund where we invest money in particular projects that will improve our business, make our fruit better....We effectively get matching funding, so collectively with SGT we've been able to buy a brand new grader for grading top fruit. This complements the one that AGA had already bought, which is mainly used for grading pears now, but it does give us a really up to date set-up, which is very necessary to position ourselves in today's very competitive market. There are an awful lot of people who are in top fruit growing, but not necessarily having too much success. The margins are very slim.

Last year David Knight produced some software called 'Making Apples Pay'...he's costed out the various areas and so you can use his software to insert your own figures and get your own results by variety. I think it's been quite educational all round - particularly for our marketeers, who have no idea what it costs to grow apples. So now you can say to them, "Well, you can't sell them for less than 35p." I certainly invite my marketeer to tell before I pick fruit whether he can sell it at a profit. If it doesn't make a profit, it'll be pulled out this autumn time... I was in east Kent last week and looking out over a vast expanse of 150 acres of arable which until recently was all top fruit.

That's how people view this job: if it doesn't pay, pull it out.

Finally, as regards the size of the labour force.

It's certainly changed quite a bit, because when we were running both farms we had quite a large regular force. We were about seven of us actually, and most of their wives would work on the farm as well - banding in and hop training, that sort of thing, fruit picking or hop picking when the time came. But we all run with the absolute minimum now: we've got two full time chaps on this farm, and Jim, who's retired, working part time, plus one or two ladies....

FARM WORKERS

Charles Forward, *born in 1906.*

Farm wages in those days in the early part of the century was only about fourteen shillings a week. People say, "Yes, but everything else was cheap", but you'd get rent for half a crown a week, and coal - I remember coal was about one and ninepence a hundredweight, best coal was about two and six. But you think of my father now: my grandfather had nine children, grandfather had fourteen shillings. Suppose he paid half a crown of that in rent - that brings you back to eleven and six. Suppose you had a hundredweight of coal - say, two bob - that brings you back to nine and six. That's less than ten pence in old money per person a week - three halfpence a day. However they done it, I don't know. They slogged it on the farm all those hours. They had large gardens in those days. And if you hadn't a large garden you had an allotment. Of course they couldn't afford to buy vegetables of any sort. If you didn't grow your own, you just didn't have any. There was no such thing as fruit in the house in my early days: oranges and lemons was just Christmas time only we ever saw anything like that. We didn't know what it was to have an orange any other part of the year.

And I remember children going to school. They was puny. They was badly fed, and there was no transport to school. I know some families from what we called Redwater - that's three or four miles away. Partly through woods and by lands and partly along the main road. The children were just over five years old walking that far to school. There was no wellington boots or mackintoshes in those days to keep the rain out if it was wet. Just had one of father's big old coats and put it over their head, or had a sack and folded it, something like that, and when we got to school no facilities for drying. I went to Sissinghurst school and your clothes just hung on a hook in an open porch.

On the farm, if it rained like cats and dogs, if the farmer hadn't got any work inside in the barn that day, you just worked out in the wet. They used to put a sack round the waist, an old one - the old jute sacks everything came in, in those days. There were no paper sacks, you see. They put another one over their shoulders and sometimes they used to wrap them round the bottom part of the legs. They'd work out in the rain till it was mealtime. At midday if it was still raining they'd take the old wet sacks off and put another lot on, and go on in the afternoon and keep on working because as soon as they stopped there was no money.

Of course most of the agricultural cottages were tied cottages. Practically all the men there, conditions were that the wife worked when it was necessary. Because lots of work women could do - haymaking, harvesting and all that - because there were no machines. It was all done by hand, you see. They used to slog in the fields as well as bring up a large family.

If men fell foul of the farmer he gave them the sack. They wouldn't get another job anywhere around here. My grandfather said you'd probably have to go out of the county to get another job. Meanwhile you've got nothing to live on at all. So they put up with all sorts of conditions, because there was no option. They couldn't do anything about it, and their home went with the job. If the job was finished, out the house you'd go, and get out quick too.

When you got too old to work you had to clear out. If you'd got a son or daughter who could take you in, well that was alright. Otherwise, up the Union you went.

Nellie Dann (nee **Piper**), *born in 1908, recorded some memories in 2000. Her father was farm foreman on Fred Winch's Brick Kiln Farm, behind High Street - status considerably above a farm labourer's, but Nellie remembers spartan living conditions.*

Dad used to get up first, early, to go out and see his cattle all right. 'Cos somebody took them out, two cows out of his herd. He used to light the kitchen fire. Then Mum used to get us up, and get us five younger ones ready for school.

Did you have water out of the tap?

Oh, no, out of a pump. Dad used to have yokes on his shoulders with two buckets. He used to go out of the house, out the garden gate and up a little path. Then there was a pump with a handle. We'd go up there and pump it.. He used to have the bucket, and put the handle over the spout. When it was full enough, he used to take it off. Then he'd put these yokes on. My biggest brother used to pick the bucket up and hook it in these yokes... He used to fill up about four, but he would fill up twice a day.

And where did you go for the toilet?
Just out, in a bucket to start with.

Brian Brew *was farming in the 1950s and 1960s, with two tied cottages.*

I never liked the idea of them. I remember once having to help my father with an eviction: I didn't enjoy that much. I don't know that he did. We knew they were going somewhere else: the Rural or Parish Council or whoever it was would immediately find them accommodation - they weren't actually turned out into the street, though their furniture was. But that was one of the aspects of farming I didn't like. And in fact farm workers I think were treated pretty badly: if you were advertising for a farm worker you could never get a reference. If a farm worker went to a farmer and asked for a reference he could never get one - the farmer would say I'm going to sack you, so it was tantamount to being sacked.

HOP PICKING

Charles Evernden *remembered picking when he was a boy before the First World War.*

It used to last for several months. I mean it used to last round to October sometimes, you know. Start early August, August, September, October. They have different types of hops, you see, one after the other, different grades. I've been out hop picking when they used to have bonfires in the hop gardens to keep you warm...

Above : Measuring hops into the pokes in the hop garden at The Bridge, Cranbrook.

Below : Cranbrook families such as the Danns, as well as East Enders, worked in the hop gardens.

Hop Picking

Everybody used to go in the old days, before the first world war. All the tradesmen's wives and everybody else used to go hop picking in those days. They had their sets, you know: they'd go to certain farmers, they'd have all the best, more select type of people, you see, sometimes than others. They wouldn't have Londoners on their farms.

But Mr Evernden remembered the Londoners with some nostalgia.

Londoners? Hop picking time, you'd find all the shops here, they'd all have wire netting cages up right over their counters and goods so they didn't get robbed... You couldn't move for hop pickers. Great fun when the police were here. Always had extra policemen in the town at hop picking time too, you know. It was lovely to go out at night time for kids, us boys you know, stand there and see these Londoners having fights, you know. Then the police used to take them off round the police station *(in Waterloo Road),* four policemen carrying a big burly man perhaps. An arm and a leg, each one got an arm and a leg, you see, and as they go along they bump him down, you know...

Remember those hop picking hopper huts at Glassenbury? ... Oh, they were primitive, proper native thatched huts they were. They were just in the wood, and you fancy Londoners coming down - they couldn't bear the dark. Being stuck in a wood, this was a field away from the road, then the wood. And they only had sort of brushwood on the earth floor, and then straw on top of that to sleep on, that sort of thing... We used to go in the woods and frighten them sometimes - they'd bolt for their lives - they'd run half a mile before they'd stop... They didn't like the country, you know - scared stiff of the dark.
The only trouble was you used to get so many fleas when the hop pickers came down... You can get rid of them now, thank goodness... *(but)* in those days, all there was, was Keatings Powders. The only thing use a candle and catch the little

devils. Sit up half the night there. If I got a flea in bed on me, I always had to get out... Everybody used to say the same: as soon as those hop pickers came down, the place was swarming with fleas. Take you months to get rid of them.

(But) some of them were alright, see. I mean some of the old Londoners, I mean they came down year after year. You knew them... Same families have been there, come there all their lifetime nearly. When they got married, they'd still come down and have their families, you know. They used to go to the same old farms, year after year. Oh yes, you got used to them.

Major Enfield, *growing hops both before and after the second world war, was one who employed only local pickers. Wage rises ultimately led him to using the picking machine instead.*

They were all local people. We used to have Londoners years ago, before we came to Cranbrook, but Londoners and local people didn't really mix... And with the Londoners you had to write to them in London, get them down, transport all the paraphernalia, with horse and wagon in those days, supply them with huts...

This was all hand picking... until the '60s when, I suppose like a lot of hop farms, it dwindled and dwindled. Well, when we started, I think it was seven bushels to the shilling - now that's a lot of work for a little money - then it got to six, and then five, and it stayed at five for a long time, but in the end I think it came to sixpence, the old sixpence, a bushel. By then it was a toss up, whether it was to keep having home pickers who were getting scarcer... so we had a hop-picking machine which employed, I suppose... about ten people on it.

Hop Picking

Bill Calcutt *of Four Wents Farm, speaking in the year 2000.*

We still have strong connections with our old Londoners and they still come down... *(In a camp)* either in hopper huts or in caravans or whatever it is. And they all, as I suppose they always have done, look upon it as a holiday... A couple of the chaps drive taxis, and they just say, "Well, it's a good time for the children for a bit, but we can earn our week's hopping money in about a day at home."

We still rely mainly on gypsies for *(hop)* training, and certainly at Finchcocks we've got a very good family. They come back and help pick them as well, drive tractors, wives on the machine and things... Most of the top fruit is picked by local people augmented by a few students, but we haven't really got student accommodation up here. I've got a cottage at Finchcocks I could put people into, but it really wants to be local people.

THE POOR

Sidney Barham *and* **Charles Evernden** *were recorded in conversation...*

S.B. There were poor people, yes, oh yes, plenty of poor people... Of course there was the relieving officer - anybody could go there and make a case. Then there was the workhouse of course... (*But people*) wouldn't go there if they could possibly help it, would they? No, they looked down on that - that was very degrading to have to go there. Never go there if they could help it. Always hoped it would never come to that... labourers that had got past work, you see, mainly...

Then there were the casuals. There were always the casual

people who go on the road, you know. The workhouse was at Hartley, which is now Hartley House, the old people's home, and you'd go up there in the afternoon and see all the casuals sitting waiting for the workhouse to open. They'd come from one workhouse to another.

C.E. Tramps in other words.

S.B. I remember my father... took me up there and showed me the place where they did the work. You see, the casuals had to do a bit of work before they were allowed out. They sat in sort of cells, open cells, with a kind of great pestle with a mortar in front of them, and a pile of stones, and they'd got to hammer these stones till they could get them through the sieve. When they'd done that they could go, you see. That was their bit of work.

C.E. And gardening. They used to have to do so much garden work too, before they left. If they stayed over the weekend, they'd got to do a bit more work Monday morning before they left.

S.B. Then there was the sight you used to see - the old roadman. Some of the inmates that were able bodied enough for it, there would be piles of roadstone along the road, ready for the road to be made up with, you see. They were big stones, might be granite, or it might be ragstone, something like that. The old chaps would come along with their long hammer and a pair of goggles to protect their eyes and they'd break these stones up, you see, sit by the roadside breaking the stones. To get them the right size.

C.E. They were there for weeks and weeks sitting by the road. They used to have a yard high and a yard wide and so many yards long, and that was an allotment they'd got to do. They got paid for so many yards they broke up...

The Poor

S.B. Yes, these old boys, a white smock they used to wear... Sit there breaking stones. And they were always ready to talk to anybody...

C.E. Of course there were big families. I know two families here: they both lost their fathers in the prime of life, like, and both left ten children, you know. Yet they survived, you know, never got into trouble either. I suppose the oldest ones had to keep the family together, like, as they grew up. Both of them, ten - one was eleven really, one unborn one - but they still survived, you know. People used to help each other more in those days - more than they do now, I think. Everybody knew each other...

S.B. There were various charitable arrangements. For instance there was the Soup Kitchen, in the Carriers Road as they call it now. In the winter, you see, there was a place where they used to make soup, and very good soup, all kind of thick barley stuff in it, you know. I've seen the children bringing these big pails and take it home to their grandparents or something like that. This soup. That used to be in the winter, in the winter time. It was really good stuff, it was very good stuff. Smelled nice too.

C.E. Yes. Neighbours would help each other too, you see. They'd take them in food and share in all that sort of thing, wouldn't they? Other people would give them clothes and help a lot.

S.B. Yes, there were charitable arrangements, you see, yes. There was the Institute, which was often made fun of, but it did a lot of good. The district visitors, the parish visitors, the ladies from the church would have a part of the parish which was theirs, and they used to go round and have a look at the old people, you know. There could be a lot of patronage in it, a lot of that, but they could do a lot of good if they were kindly disposed... There used to be a funny old lady that Mr Evernden would know, Miss Alice Wood. She was one of the district visitors, and she was one of the sort - she was kindly but she was very inquisitive at the same time. She'd want to know all about you, you know, that kind of thing...

C.E. Church societies a lot, Blanket Clubs and different clubs like that. There were a lot of clubs, weren't there?... As I say, Lord Cranbrook, they used to do a lot, you know.

S.B. One thing that I remember with regard to Hemsted, there was quite an institution over there, the ladies used to present scarlet cloaks to the schoolchildren at Christmas. I don't know what the boys got, but the girls used to have these things. You always knew Benenden because they were walking about with these sort of Red Riding Hood cloaks on, you know. They were given by the Cranbrooks.

C.E. Always used to give them a big joint at Christmas, practically everybody on the estate, didn't they? Everybody was fed well. And when there was illness there, they were ever so good. You'd think these ladies, Lady Cranbrook and the rest of them, they took a great interest in social affairs, local you know, and they looked after - they knew all the illnesses and hardships there was in the district, I think.

S.B. And of course there was the parish doctor, you see. If you were a poor person, you could have the parish doctor. The parish doctor would tend to you, and they were very good, some of those... Dr Harris, he was very good to old people like that: poor people... Do what he could for them.

ROAD AND RAIL

Charles Forward, *recollecting the very early years of the 20th century.*

Angley Road was just - we used to call it Back Lane - a narrow winding lane from Wilsley coming out at the top. And from Courtstile apart from the little lodge gate to Angley Park there was no houses whatever till you got to where Mr Savory's houses are: no houses, simply fields on either side. And rather more parkland on the Angley School side...

Occasionally an old traction engine would come along, of course - steam engine, we used to call them traction engines. It would be pulling three trucks - they used to haul stones for roadmaking and bricks and that sort of thing, you see. They would go puffing along, or an old steam engine sometimes with a horse wagon behind it. And of course in those days there was heaps of what we call roadside ponds which have all been filled in now - because these old engines they used an enormous lot of water. They used to drop their hosepipe in these roadside ponds and suck up and replenish their tanks, you see. They didn't go very far before they had to replenish the tanks again. Now and again you'd see a notice on the ponds, "No water to be drawn from this pond". It was someone's private but, if there was nobody about and they needed it, of course the pump used to be pushed through the hedge and down in the pond and they'd fill up again.

Of course people often say now the motor car has taken the place of the horse... There was horses on the farms - you'd often see them on the road. Three horse or two horse or one horse teams hauling stuff from farm to farm or perhaps going to the station - you see, you used the railway to bring the stuff.

Some of the tradesmen had horses. The butcher and the baker they had two-wheeled traps and the coalman had a horse in a flat trolley for coal. The miller would come round with a horse and wagon, and there was the brewers' drays. Of course some of the large country houses had their coaches - town-going coach, about two horses each. A few of the middle class houses here and there might have a horse, but of course a horse is not like a motor car - if they'd got a horse they had to have a man to look after it. Apart from that, people got about by foot and bicycle - there was no other means of transport.

Tom East *moved to Cranbrook in 1911. After serving in the first world war, he joined the Maidstone and District Bus Company in 1920. In June, 2000, a few weeks short of his hundredth birthday, he answered questions at length.*

When you joined in 1920, what sort of buses were they?

Solid tyres and open tops. Double deckers, open tops. Charabancs we called them then.

What colour were they?

Green. Maidstone and District always have been green.

What route did they follow?

When I first went up there, I was Gillingham. Two years I was at Gillingham, and we ran to Sittingbourne, Gillingham, Maidstone, most of the times. Then they gradually extended and extended it, they came right over to Hastings. They used to run to Hawkhurst sometime, that was service 5. Service 8 was Hawkhurst to Hastings - that was only open in the summer time. Service 5 came to Cranbrook. I was transferred to Hawkhurst depot when I'd been with the company for about four years then. It was opened as a branch to Brighton then,

Road and Rail

Hawkhurst to Brighton... They had solitary buses stationed here and there. At Cranbrook, only one bus at Cranbrook, there was then.

How often did that run?

Every hour. Cranbrook to Maidstone.

Could you get to Tunbridge Wells from Cranbrook?

Not then, no. Red Cars, the auto cars, opened up to the Tunbridge Wells and Maidstone area. Our people bought them out... In the end there was an hourly service. Hourly to Maidstone. Hourly to Tunbridge Wells.... I was transferred back to Hawkhurst then, where there was an hourly service to Brighton. Two different routes to Tunbridge Wells, 80 and 84. 84 was to Tunbridge Wells right through Wadhurst and Flimwell. 80 was the one through Ticehurst and Wadhurst.

When you first started, what was the fare from Cranbrook to Maidstone?

Half a crown return. One and ten single. Eightpence return from Cranbrook to Hawkhurst. Sixpence single. A lot of money in those days. Used to be four shillings to Hastings.

Were they always double decker buses, or did you have some single decker buses?

We had the single decker buses... Some of them used to have a canopy over the top. You could pull it all the way back, like these cars do. Hook it all round the back. If it rained, we had to come out and hook it all the way along. A big strap to pull it tight, and then hook it all the way along the side in wet weather. Charabancs they called them.

Above : the carrier's cart in Waterloo Road.

*Below : one of the first motor buses, before World War I.
The driver is Mr. F. Piper.*

41

I remember at Hastings, when I was a conductor, a woman got on there. She always came out of Battle. She was always telling people what the grand days felt like. One day she got on this ordinary coach with an open top. She sat there awhile, she says: "Scuse me," she says, "Close the window."
I says, "Close the window, why? We got no windows here."
"There's a terrible draught," she says.
I says, "You're sitting in the open air."
She put *(out)* her hand... "Well, I never did!" she says.

Cranbrook's station at Hartley, on the branch line to Hawkhurst, was working from 1893 until 1961.
David Wickham *describes some of its effects on Cranbrook.*

They had special hop-picking trains... they used to come and arrive at the station with all their belongings and we used to have to go along with our tractor and trailer and bring them all along to the farm. They used to bring their goods down in one of those pushcart sort of things, home made, box on wheels, a huge great box with handles on. Or old prams were the thing. And the porters used to curse... with these things, carrying them in and out of the carriages. Plenty of cockney language flying around!

The line was used by farmers for taking hops to London and taking fruit, which was obviously a very direct line to what it was before. Before it went by horse and wagon to Maidstone - an all day job. Fruit of course used to go up, and things like flowers - there were one or two nurseries round here. Plants, flowers, all sorts of produce like that... small quantities... mushrooms.

And of course we used it. We used to have the shoddy come down, which was woollen waste from the mills from West Yorkshire - Heckmondwyke? A truckful of this loose shoddy which is all the waste from the factories, and was spread out on the hops... We had fertiliser came in there sometimes.

But farmers were not the only users of the line.

There were lots of people who wanted to go up to London. A train at eight o'clock was the first one... We used to go up to see the hops in London... It used to time very nicely at Paddock Wood with the London train from Ashford; the school children used to go to Paddock Wood and Tonbridge - it was used a lot by school children.

The railway could be a nuisance to neighbouring farmers.

We had some dry summers and of course coming up to the station here it was all uphill - one in five hundred, or whatever it was... and the train had to get on, and it threw sparks out and it set the herbage along the railway line alight, and we were growing corn in the field next door. Several times this happened, and we had to go out, a rush to get out and beat the flames. It used to burn just the grass - it was very dry. Once it got over the fence and into the crop we didn't know if they would give compensation, we didn't stop to find out... And then we'd go down to the stationmaster, and he'd say, "Oh, yes?"... But the railway had no staff: I mean, the porter wouldn't help, the platelayer was usually in the other direction, so we had to do it ourselves. It was usually only when they had to stoke up the oven to get that extra bit of pull up the incline... Coming up here was quite a pull - I know it was only gradual, but it was enough to make the whole thing grunt.

AMUSEMENTS AND ENTERTAINMENTS

Sidney Barham, *born in 1887, was the son of a humble but serious, self-improving late Victorian Cranbrook father.*

What little entertainments were going, I suppose he used to go to them. But there were very few: mostly concerts and that kind of thing you'd go to... We were all brought up to chapel, you see - and so was my uncle, a different chapel. There used to be things going on there, sacred concerts and things like that... The organist of the church, old Tommy Francis, was also a music teacher. He used to arrange oratorios. I remember once father thought it would be a good idea if I learned a bit of music, so he entered me to go to the rehearsals for Judas Maccabaeus... It was down at what we called the coffee tavern down at the bridge - but it's now the Working Men's club... I did get to learn some of the choruses and can still remember them. And I know that he once took me to see Mendelssohn's Elijah. But we didn't go to many, not posh affairs of that sort...

Then my father was a member and very interested in the local Literary Association, which had a reading room and lending library for members, you see, in Vestry Hall. And my uncle was the same. They used to go up there for the newspapers and he used to be on the committee of that, and we had the privilege of once a week going up in the little room in the tower of Vestry Hall, the tower room as it was called, and there was a library up there, and we changed books up there. I got a lot of my information and education up there. Old fashioned, many of them, but they were quite good.

(In reply to a question asking who went to the Literary Society.) Well, decent people. When I say decent people,

trades people and some of the better sort of artisans... not the farm labourers, oh no... I don't remember many ladies going, I don't think my mother ever went... There were these lectures arranged, you see - public lectures where you could pay to go in and see. They were quite popular - some were and some weren't...

I heard a lecture in the very early days of the X-rays. A gentleman at Sissinghurst, Captain Wilson-Knowle - he was a retired naval man, I imagine - was an experimental scientist and he experimented in X-rays, or Roentgen rays they used to call them in the early days, you know. He had a laboratory down there and works of various kinds and he gave a lecture to the Literary Association... he went through the whole rigmarole. At one stage he demonstrated: he had a screen up there, and the curate, who was a bit of a sport, went up there and knelt in front of the thing, and we saw the ghostly figure of the curate's backbone. That was the climax of the exhibition, as it were. But he'd given us a lot of information in advance, all about fluorescence and that sort of thing. And that was quite advanced, wasn't it?...

But that was about the limit in what we went to in the way of shows. They used occasionally to have a travelling theatre used to come here. Linington and Becket, they used to come with... posters and cowboys and all that sort of thing. Father took me once to one of them - only once. A thing called Our Flat... a comedy of some sort, farce I suppose really. But he wouldn't have wasted his money on anything like that normally, not my father wouldn't. Oh no.

Charles Evernden, *born in 1899, recalled a boyhood before the First World War.*

Have you ever done window tapping?...You used to have a nice big button on a thread hanging up with a pin, you see, and the

Amusements and Entertainments

thread would go across to the other side of the road somewhere. You just kept tapping and tapping the window - then they came out. Or pull on the knockers, that sort of thing. But never got nothing serious, not in those days...

Another little game we used to play when we was boys at school. They always kept sheep in the churchyard - we used to have to go through the churchyard to school, you know. When you was up to about twelve or thirteen, you know... you used to creep up behind the tombstones and grab hold of a sheep's leg and try to hold one, you know - see who could hold it longest. And of course when you're that age, you're not strong enough to hold a sheep long, when you get a full grown sheep kicking, you know. But it used to be great fun. Quite harmless fun, you know, no danger in it. Never used to be like vandals are nowadays...

Magic lantern, that was about the only excitement you got in those days - there was no cinemas... I remember, if you saw a barrel organ come along, the excitement, you know: a monkey on one of these organs, and performing bear. And they put up at the old Bird in Hand - that was a sort of pub just down below us *(at the corner of Stone Street and Waterloo Road)*, and that was a sort of doss house too. We used to slip up there to try to see this performing bear and this monkey dressed up, you know. That was exciting...

You amused yourself, though. I mean, at school, you had your season when you had marbles, you had another season when you had tip cat, and another one was hoops in the winter time... All these different games, and bows and arrows... Men used to play goal running: they used to run miles at night time, you know, after a day's work... All the villages round here used to have goal running clubs...

I'll tell you one thing I used to do though, Saturdays - when we was boys, used to go and earn a shilling, Saturday. Used to go beating - pheasant shoots, you see. They'd hire us boys - so many boys and so many men... First perhaps you'd have an hour or two standing outside the wood - they'd be posted all along, beaters, wood boys - and you had to keep tapping, making a noise, so the birds wouldn't come out, you see... The guns would be in the fields, each side of the woods, and as soon as they started to drive, you'd join in and go through the wood, driving the birds out, you see. Get a shilling for that and bread and cheese, and some lemonade perhaps or beer for the grown-ups, you see. Great excitement, that was. One man here, he was an auctioneer, so he bought a lot of ex-hunting coats for sale sometimes. He used to hold these sales... so we used to put these scarlet jackets on, so we'd show up. Pretty proud when we'd got a scarlet jacket on, and got a shilling as well, you know, for a day's beating.

Nick Metson's *memories go back to a Cranbrook boyhood in the 1920s and early 1930s.*

The old Cranbrook cinema, down in the Tanyard, was like a big old army hut, that probably was an army hut. We had it as a cinema between the wars, when I was a boy. To give you the rake - you know, the tilt - it was built with the front of it on the ground and on concrete pillars of varying heights, so that it sloped. At the front was a sort of appendage which was the stage with a screen. At the back of it - it was like a hut on stilts, with a ladder up to it, that had the projector in. For heating, it had a big old Tortoise stove, and that was on the side nearest the River Crane, with a tin chimney that came out the side and up. In the winter, when chestnuts were about, we used to go and get a pocketful of chestnuts, and go to the pictures on a Saturday night - or on a Wednesday - and put all the chestnuts on the top of the old Tortoise stove, and cook chestnuts while we were watching the pictures.

Amusements and Entertainments

Underneath it some of the Tanyard boys, they had a gang - the boys used to form gangs - they had their headquarters underneath the cinema in amongst the concrete piles.

When they showed the films, they used to have films going here, and at the Victoria Hall in Hawkhurst. They used to have a sort of 'moving cinema'. You used to have two films - the main film and the second film - always. If they were showing the main film here, they would be showing the second film at Victoria Hall in Hawkhurst. When this film finished, they used to whip it off the projector, and there would be an interval. There was a motorbike and sidecar there - a chap named Vic Gell, who worked for a milk round in the daytime, but he used to do this as an extra job at night. He used to race with the old motorbike and sidecar to Hawkhurst, with the film, and bring back the film that they'd been showing. So the interval lasted as long as it took him to get to Hawkhurst and back, and then we had the second film going.

It had a piano, because it wasn't Talkies: it was all silent, a lady playing the piano. I can't think what her name is. I always remember her hair was drawn back in a bun, and she used to play the piano.

When there was the cowboys, then there was the 'da-diddley-da' and so forth. We all used to chuck orange peel at the villain when he came on the screen. We used to have a whale of a time there.

Edward Ryan's *boyhood memories are of the 1930s.*

Cranbrook was different then. There wasn't the traffic in the street. Where the cinema was, and upward, that was a playground. We all played games in the street. Hoops and tops the boys had, never ball games - that wasn't allowed. The girls

Amusements and Entertainments

had skipping ropes and did hop-scotch. In the road itself. Occasionally a car would come and it would hoot, and you would just get out of the way. But all that finished in the '30s because the traffic increased. In the early '30s I remember, '30, '31, we all played in the street until it was time to go in, for an hour or two of a night.

We played football in Ball Field, and cricket for school. It was frowned on playing games on a Sunday. That was very bad.

We used to go to Sunday School at the Congregational Church on a Sunday, and afterwards we all went for a walk in Cranbrook woods, like everybody did in those days. Cranbrook woods was used much more then than it is now. People would get dressed up in their Sunday best, just to walk through the woods in the afternoon, or other places.

There was also, on a Wednesday night in the winter, what we called the 'Amen' meetings. That was a church service at the Bull room, which is now offices. You know where the Bull pub was? Pastor Basset came from Smarden on a Wednesday night and held a service there. Hymn singing and whatnot, it was rather nice. It was in the warm; you were allowed to go out. But only in the winter time. They called it the 'Amen' meeting because there was a little old man, a peculiar man called Ebbie Curtis, he used to sit at the front and every few minutes he'd say "Amen". So children called it the 'Amen' meeting. That was one of the pursuits...

(*In addition to the cinema*) there was also the theatre which came occasionally to Cranbrook. It was down Wilkes' field: you've got some cottages, which was once a pub called The Spotted Dog - well, next to that was a field, which the school has now. Well, that was the field, and fairs used to come there and circuses which you don't even see now.... It was a portable theatre. It was a wooden structure, with a grass floor, and a

Amusements and Entertainments

coke brazier going in the middle of the gangway. And they used to perform all plays, which you could go and see for fourpence.

The last time they came to Cranbrook was 1937. They used to tour all the villages round here, from one village to another. They'd stay at Cranbrook for about six weeks, then they'd come back after another couple of years. They had lorries and things like that: they lived in caravans. I saw 'Maria Martin and Murder in the Red Barn'. I saw 'The Mistletoe Bough'. And of course there was always 'Sweeney Todd the Barber', which frightened the life out of everybody. In fact they did any Victorian play they could put on. They could learn those plays off by heart, and with a short bit of rehearsing they had the play ready for the evening.

When the war came, they weren't able to carry on, because of the blackout. That finished it for ever.

Rodney Dann *recalls the leisure activities of young people shortly before the Beatles era.*

Activities and amusements? Not so different from today. But we were fortunate to have the Regal cinema - two showings a week. No youth clubs. But cafes, coffee bars: the Weald Restaurant where Anderson's the butcher's is now, and another one on the corner of Waterloo Road - Ron's Caff, behind the junk shop... Also that was the time when traditional jazz was in its heyday: we used to go down by coach to Hastings every Saturday, where there was a good following - the Dolphins were the local band. And for a while we had our own jazz band in the old ballroom above Cranbrook Engineering...

Most Saturday nights there was a dance - either in Vestry Hall or Drill Hall or in one of the villages around. Bands - Doris

Amusements and Entertainments

Pullen's and others... The village lads would come in and muscle in on our local girls, and we'd do the same. There was the occasional punch-up...

It was the era of the Teds. I'd got the drainpipe trousers. We couldn't afford to buy, but with Mum's sewing machine we'd take the seams in. And the long jacket and Eton suedes with thick crepe soles, bootlace tie, Tony Curtis hair and D.A. at the back - we were Jack the Lads.

As for the Lasses, **Pat Duxbury**, *who left school in 1952 at seventeen and then worked for three years at Shipman's, the Stone Street chemist's, recalls the times with fondness.*

Great fun. Lots of dancing - we were always dancing: Vestry Hall mostly, and in the rooms above the garage - some rooms at the top, where we did Old Time Dancing with Mr Butler. And somehow, though we'd no transport except bikes, go to the villages to dances there. My girl friend said they all used to go off on bikes and the one that had the rear light was last and the one that had the front light was the first. We were in CODS and the social side of CODS where we did a lot of square dancing and went to the other villages to teach square dancing and the Eightsome Reel...

There always seemed to be something you could do - lots more than there appears to be now. We went everywhere on cycles. We used to slip up to Bedgebury and swim in the lake, by the school - terribly illegal, terribly dangerous - the water lilies there are lethal. Quite a lot of sport. I helped the scoring with the cricket team: not the first eleven (the first eleven had Mr Larkin) - we were the second eleven, mind you. And then when I left school I couldn't go any more, because I worked Saturdays - so I did the Wednesday shopkeepers team... Very nice they were, very gentle.

Above : The Regal Cinema.

Below : The Crown Inn.

WORLD WAR TWO

Geoff Apps *was aged six when war began. He recalled his days at the Elementary School.*

They had paper crosses on the windows. You had to carry your gas mask wherever you went. In fact in the beginning you had to sit there and work in them. They made your face very red and hot, but it was something you had to get used to. It was to make you used to breathing with them, not to worry about putting them on... We used to laugh at each other: you imagine, a black face looking at you, with a long snout on the front.

(But...) up at Hartley, down at Tubslake - the beginning of the war - when all the big raids were going over, he spotted us walking along the road, decided he didn't like the look of us, so he just came down and machine-gunned us and we had to dive into the ditch.

(At school) one of the things we had to do was to collect newspapers or paper. They had it like the army - if you collected so much, you became a Corporal, and so much more and you became a Sergeant, and worked your way up. Latter part when I was there I was a steward on the dinner thing, for the infants. There came an air raid warning once, and of course they all dived underneath the desks. We were too big to dive under their little desks, so we dived into a corner, into what looked like a solid wendy house. We were sitting there, looked up and we could see the ceiling. There was no roof to this wendy house at all - so it was a lot of good if anything had happened. It was only doodlebugs at that time, so it was an unlikely chance.

(But) if one doodlebug had dropped twelve hours earlier, I wouldn't be here. The twelve hours? We were all playing on a bridge in Henniker up at Hartley - there was a big old bridge. We were playing on it at eight o'clock one night: next morning at eight o'clock there was a doodlebug landed smack on it.

I can remember lying in bed at night and listening to the drone as they came over. Then during hop picking time watching them all come over, and the battles going on up above you. Used to stand there and watch it. We never thought anything about the shells dropping down...

We were allowed to look at the *(crash)* sites. There used to be one chappie guarding it to start off with, but if they removed everything which was deadly, then they'd leave it alone and wait for the rest of the removal people to come along. Of course during that time you were there scavenging. Perspex was the main thing you were looking for. Used to make rings out of it, or table napkins. Heated it, drilled it, filed it. It was so new, you see.

For **Brigid Longley**, *the Battle of Britain took place in her teenage years.*

Well, yes, it was quite exciting. Quite a bit of machine-gunning and so on. In holidays with various friends aged about fourteen we all got on bicycles and hoped to be the first people on the scene of crashed fighters and possibly capture a German. But we never were...

I remember when I was perhaps fifteen being approached by someone (I don't know whether from Civil Defence or who) who said they were organising young people to help if the Germans came. We really thought the Germans probably would come. And everyone was to stay in their houses until they were told to come out and young people were to go up and down behind the streets and see that everybody had food and where anyone needed any medical attention.... I've not found anyone else who remembers being asked: all I had to prove that it had ever happened was an enormous tin opener with which I was going to open huge tins of bully beef or something. Which was going to be stored somewhere behind the south side of High Street - I think possibly at Corn Hall but I'm not sure. As it never happened, mercifully.

But **Doris Dapson,** *very young though she was, experienced real action.*

Well, the Battle of Britain was on in 1940, and of course most of it was on while we were hop picking. And we went to the Enfields' *(farm at)* Goddards Green every year to pick hops, but that year we had to go to farms at Goudhurst as well to pick, because nobody would pick the hops. And I can remember sheltering in a barn with my grandmother and my mother and the raid was going on overhead and there was a barrage balloon on fire. And as we went back to the hop garden we saw the pilot hanging dead in one of the trees. I think it was one of ours....

And I can remember this German came and started to machine gun the hop garden. And I can remember my father pushing me to the ground to protect me, and that's all I can remember of it really...

Major Enfield *remained on the farm during the war, and was a member of the Home Guard.*

Major Saunders was the *(senior)* officer - he was very nice - we got on with him very well. We had a bank manager as our

Cranbrook Volunteers in the Second World War.

Above : Civil Defence First Aid Point.

Below : Cranbrook Home Guard.

division officer - you could polish all your things up and your clothes up, and if he said you get down in the mud, that's what you did.

We had duties. I think it was once a month in the Drill Hall. And we used to go down to Folkestone - carried down there by Tippen's lorry, an open back lorry - and they used to take us down there and we used to guard the pier, what was left of the pier. There was a tunnel that went through to Dover, a railway tunnel, and we had to guard that one... We had a headquarters there, but it was just to relieve the people that were down there, to give them a break. We used to go down there with our rifles, loaded rifles it was. We were told to shoot people and shoot them at the legs for a start: they said shoot them at the legs, but of course we never had to use it. What we used to do when the fly bombs came over, we used to take potshots at them with rifles: that was more, I think, it was more fun than anything else - it was something different. But I don't think we ever hit one of them.

CHURCH AND CHAPEL

St Dunstan's Church, St Theodore's, the Congregational Church, Providence Chapel and the Baptist Chapel all played an important part in the life of Cranbrook in the 20th century.

In 1900, funerals were still held in the churchyard, and made a big impression on the young **Sidney Barham.**

There's one aspect of life has changed, the coming of the cemetery. Now when I was a boy, see, the school was the other side of the churchyard and all the burials were in the churchyard, you see, in those days. So we were always seeing that happening. There was also the passing bell. Originally it had been during the actual dying of a person to call for prayers, but it wasn't that now, of course. They would have the bell after the death. You see, it was all a sort of mystic affair, death was. I mean, we often used to see it in the school playground, we'd see the little group in the churchyard, with the vicar with his surplice and the mourners and that standing around at the funeral, you see.

The curious thing was that even the most furious Dissenters would have the bell, although it was a Catholic idea really, to ring for prayers for the departing, but it had lost that. But you didn't feel you were properly dead unless you had the proper bell. I can see once my grandfather - a relative had died at Sissinghurst, and he came tearing along the road. Mother said, "What's the matter with so-and-so?" " Oh, so-and-so has passed away, I'm going to order the bell"... They were all Calvinists and that, nothing to do with the church at all, but they must have the bell. They rationalized it, they said, "Well, it's so useful to warn the living, you see", but of course it wasn't that really, it was a sort of feeling that you must have the bell or you're not properly dead.

For centuries there had been differences between church and chapel. Sidney Barham describes how these flared up in 1902.

If you were church, you were Tory, you see, but if you were chapel, you were a Liberal. That made all the difference. It was a fact of history, you see, it had always been like that. In the '90s it didn't matter so much, but when you see the trouble that arose with the Balfour Education Bill in 1902, that's when the cat was put on all the monster pigeons. See, as I told you, although we were Dissenters, we went to the church school and we were taught all in the church school, nobody objected to it at all, but when the question came of a new act coming along, Balfour's Education Bill, it put the church schools right on the rates. That upset all the Dissenters, you see, they were all in arms about it... I remember we had a fresh minister arrive, and he was a great seller, came to our house on one occasion, and he told us all about this terrible thing that was going to happen, you know, all our liberties were going to be at stake... They had a great series of public meetings, and they used to arrange coaches and charabancs to take protesters to the various villages, and there would be these orators getting up there. I remember old Bill Nash... of course he was a terrific Liberal, he used to say, "This irrequitious Balfour bill, this irrequitious Balfour bill."

Sidney Barham also describes the strong feelings against Roman Catholics early in the century.

A lot of very bigoted Protestants too in those days. I heard my mother talk about that. There used to be quite a meeting of them at Mr Walters', the little stationer's shop in Stone Street, there was one or two Nashes or something used to come there and argue about it. I heard her say that one man said the Catholics would be coming back some day, and he said, "What, that bloody whore?"...What they'd say now to having a Catholic church here I don't know. At the National School there used to be a little handful of Catholics, they used to come in late, and they didn't get into classes until we had finished.

There was a sergeant-major of the Volunteers, Sergeant-Major Harris, he had a Catholic wife, you know, his boys used to be withdrawn from school, and there was a tale about he had a little girl who died, and they put pennies on her eyes. Whether it was to pay her purgatory fees or whether it was just to keep her eyelids stuck... And there was one lady in Mrs Stokes's shop, Miss Button, and she was a Catholic, she used to go to Goudhurst, you know, that was the only chapel round here in those days... and we used to look on her with awe, almost with dread. Very nice lady really, but she was a Catholic... The

Church and Chapel

Protestant Alliance used to arrange lectures here, and all the Protestants used to go to these. Lantern lectures all about the martyrs - I remember one lantern show we had "Some Famous Bonfires, Bones, Bibles and Brave Men".

After the First World War, the influence of the churches began to fade, as did the disagreements between them. But in the 1930s many people still went to church.

Major Enfield *was choirboy, server, bellringer and then sidesman at St Dunstan's for fifty years beginning in the 1930s.*

We had quite a good choir, and in those days we used the old vestry which is now gone... We had a procession every Sunday. Some of the banners we carried weren't very easy to manage, because they were free hanging on a pole, and the cross members were free, so they swayed all over the place, and the only way you could see where you were going was to look at the people's heels in front of you. If you lifted them up, took them too high, you hit the candelabra. Oh, we had a good choir there twice a Sunday. It was different in those days. People went to church in those days, you had a suit on, everything was different. Whether it's for the better or not, of course...

I can remember one day when we had a choir practice, I didn't go to the practice because we had the same hymns over and over again. So I thought, "I'm going to miss choir practice." When Sunday came I went on to the vestry and got dressed up in the cassocks and that; the organist said, "Where are you going?" I said, "I'm going to sing in the choir." He said, "You didn't come to practice, so you can't come to church," and he told me to go home. Which I took my things off and went home. And I'm afraid it was a long time before I went back again. Because it was the same service we had every time.

Above : The East Window of St Dunstan's Church, Cranbrook's Memorial to Queen Victoria 1906.

Below : Interior, Providence Chapel, in use until the 1960s.

Church and Chapel

Bell-ringing? It was before they were rehung, they were very heavy, the tenor was 25 hundredweight, and they were on wooden headstocks , so you not only swung the bell, you swung the headstock. There was no counter-balance on them, so they were really hard work. But I did help with the Victory Peal, after the war, which was three and a half hours ringing without stopping, and we got through it all right. We couldn't ring at all during the war. The only time when I did ring, when we used to have practices and the bells being tied up with a piece of leather, and the clapper tied up. Well, one of them came loose one day, and of course it made it ring, and this was a sign for invasion, if the church bells rang, so of course we panicked a bit and this made things worse. You can't set them up when you want to, you've got to balance them just right, but eventually we overcame it .

We had Cyril Butler who lived in the church house - what is now Church House, and he lived there and looked after the boiler and the church; he was verger, he looked after all the funerals and weddings . We used to go down there, he used to make us cups of tea... I think it helped us to go to church because we was always welcomed in there.

We got on well with Canon Ashley Brown. We were only boys, but because we went to church he got to know the two little boys which were us, and used to offer us plums and, "Come round to the vicarage after the service and have a few plums." We had a number of curates in my time, in fact I was married there by a curate - and afterwards I don't know what happened to him, I think he left the church. When he was in church, he was in church - he did everything right. Douglas Remington, he was.

We got on because he used to run the Youth Club. I used to belong to St Dunstan's Youth Club and that was a church thing, so it brought us all together.. We used to meet in Baker's, what used to be the Fire Station at Baker's Cross, every Sunday. But if you didn't go to church you couldn't go to the club. There were about twenty of us, boys and girls. When the girls finished their Red Cross sessions we used to come up there, we had a gramophone, we used to play dance records, things like that... taught ourselves to dance a lot of the time. We used to go and play tennis at Old Cloth Hall, I think it was.

Peter Jempson *speaks of his father's connection with Providence Chapel, where he was married in 1934, and of his own memories of it during and just after the war.*

Providence Chapel was going strong when I came along. When I was old enough I went to the Sunday school there in the basement or undercroft of it, along with quite a lot of other Cranbrookians. My mother played the organ there, the old harmonium, and I think they rather fell out, and we then transferred our allegiance to the Congregational Church, where my mother was again organist and superintendent of the Sunday School, but that was after the end of the war, I think.

Providence Chapel was a Baptist Chapel. It had this total immersion sort of pool as it were, which is still there, and I certainly remember when I was quite young seeing my maternal grandfather baptize somebody by total immersion. Yes, it wasn't like the sort of 'stand up and get dunked' version in St Dunstan's, this was a proper bath! My father or my grandfather, whoever was doing the baptizing used to wear waders, fishermen's waders.

Of course, there was the other Baptist Chapel at St David's Bridge. I don't know how or why they developed differently , but they were quite separate churches and both had their congregations when I was growing up in Cranbrook. Whether the one on the Hill is older and the need for a bigger church led

Church and Chapel

to some breakaway faction and led to Providence Chapel being built. That was quite a day, wasn't it! Dad reckoned it was the first prefabricated building. They built it in London somewhere, brought it down by section in carts.

Daphne Russell *has lived in the Weald all her life, but settled in Cranbrook when her children were young, and joined the Congregational Church.*

When I moved from Benenden to Cranbrook I sent my children to the Congregational Church and obviously went there myself. At that time there was a big congregation there and also a great number of children. There were various different classes, in fact at one time, when I first started teaching Sunday School, there was eight Sunday School classes in one room, so it was bedlam. There was getting on for about 150 children in various groups and during that time I did teach the girl Jucos, the Junior Covenanters. They were a national organization, and we used to go on holidays to various places and I used to take my holidays there. I did that for about six years...At that time also the boy Jucos gave up because there was Sunday football coming in. But the older Covenanters still went there.

I've been in the Cranbrook Congregational Church now for about thirty years. It's changed a lot because a lot of the mainstays at that time moved on to other jobs in other parts of the country, and there weren't the talented people coming along. And so the congregation has gone right down actually and at the moment it's a very old congregation. In fact I'm one of the youngest members. The Congregational Church is run by the congregation. It has deacons who are a committee that run the church, treasurer, secretary etc, and we look after both the building and helping our local minister to run the services. Sometimes we help during the services, like helping with Holy Communion, taking the glasses and the bread around.

PRIMARY SCHOOLS

Schools always play a large part in the life of any community, and with five schools in the parish, education is a major industry in Cranbrook. Many of our interviews included reminiscences about school days.

The Primary School was founded in the early 19th century as a National School and is still a church foundation today. It moved from the old building on the Ball Field to its present site in 1985.

Sidney Barham *remembers religious education at the National School early in the century.*

Of course the National Schools were run by the Church. We were taught the catechism and all that kind of thing. The vicar or the curate used to come in and give us scripture lessons on the Gospels and all that kind of thing, you see. We were taught the Catechism and the Prayer Book in the ecclesiastical year. Although of course we were not conformists, but there was never any pressure put on us about it. But we did have religious lessons and prayers; we could have been withdrawn if we'd really cared about it. The only children that were withdrawn were the little handful of Roman Catholics. They used to come in late, and stand and wait until the scripture was over, you see, then they'd come in.

But we used to go, all my cousins and that, they were all chapel people of various sorts, they all went to the church school; went through the church business and all that kind of thing. "By baptism we were made a Member of Christ, the Child of God, an Inheritor of the Kingdom of Heaven." You know, they had to recite all that rigmarole.

I remember being terrified as a small boy in the infants' school, suddenly the teacher said, "Rehearse the articles of thy belief!" I thought, "Good gracious, what have I got to do?" But it wasn't me. A little girl piped up one side. That was funny, I've never forgotten that. But I've never regretted going through that sort of education, the religious side. I knew all along that it wasn't right, let's say that I didn't belong to all that, but that didn't make any difference. See, I was brought up with the Congregational Church, father was a Congregationalist, that sort of thing, and I had to go to Sunday School and so forth. But I much preferred what I learned in Day School, the Old Testament , than what I learnt in Sunday School.

Sidney Barham also has memories of discipline at the National School.

It was straightforward, it wasn't inhuman or anything like that. Because you could get a good old whacking; I never did get a whacking from the headmaster but he could do it. He did do it, on our rears as you might say, held them down on his knee and all that kind of thing. Oh, yes, he could do that. But I escaped all that. I was only caned once, and that was at the infants' school, and I'll never forget the old lady, the old governess that did that. I'd been laughing in the class or something, I'd been reproved and I hadn't heard it, so the teacher made me come and stand out, you see, and I suppose the headmistress saw me standing there . "What had I done?" And I told her. "Come out and hold your hand out," you see. I thought the end of the world had come. It was a long time before she got me to put my hand out, and I got this one whack, just a whack, you know. But you know I was absolutely broken down over that for days and days after that.

I had one or two escapes. I really owe the master, I think the mercy of the master for not inflicting it. I remember once, it was in winter time, snowy, we'd just come out of school in the

Primary Schools

morning, going home to dinner, and there was a bigger boy who said, "Come on, let's go and snowball the girls." The girls had a playground of their own, the girls that had dinner there, that didn't go home. We snowballed the girls, you see, for a bit of fun, and I thought no more about it, and in the afternoon the headmaster was very severe about this snowballing, and he called out this big boy and he gave him the cane, and he had another one with him, but I couldn't see who it was. He probably had seen, but he knew I'd been got up there with the other boy and he wasn't going to punish me for that.

In one of the earlier classes we'd done very badly in some subject... and we were all called out in a row, the delinquents, and the headmaster was sent for... and it was understood we were all going to be caned. But he had a good look at us and was very severe and that was all. It's like waiting to be executed, you know, and then having a reprieve.

My parents approved of the discipline. They didn't believe in severe punishment, but they wouldn't tolerate any sort of slackness... But there was this Miss Sutherland, the infants' teacher, she had rather a reputation of being a martinet, and one or two things she used to do which weren't very good. There was a dark cupboard underneath a sort of gallery there where there were steps going up with seats, and there was a cupboard underneath and she used to put kids in there, you see. The story is that on one occasion she put someone in there and forgot about putting them there... She was alright really, she'd got that way with her...There was always a procession to meet Miss Sutherland. She used to live across the field, one of the Windmill Cottages... They'd all go out in a flock and accompany her to the school. She was quite genial like that.

By the time **Major Enfield** *came to the school in the 1930s, the building was becoming seriously out of date in its facilities. It was also catering for children up to the age of 14.*

Primary Schools

We moved to Cranbrook, my father took another farm in Cranbrook. Well, the school, the only one at the time was the primary school. I'm afraid my father said "No. I've paid enough for you...so you must make your own way in the primary school." Well, this was a very behind school, because there was no electrics. There was water but there was one wash hand basin for the whole school. We had candles on the desks, and in the winter, when it was dark, they could only read us stories. So our education wasn't really up to standard as it should have been.

The head teacher there was a Mr Chapman. He used to take the boys, his wife, who was a governess, used to take the girls, so the boys did the woodwork, the girls did the sewing. We joined in with the girls until it got dark in the evening, where we had to revert back to the candlelight, and had to sit by the fire and listen to the stories told by the headmaster. And that was my education right up till I was fourteen. We never got anything more advanced.

Pat Duxbury *started at the school in 1940; she recalls school life during the Second World War.*

Miss Smith was our first teacher - when we had the lovely nap in the afternoon... They had beds that they unfolded, and they all went and lay down. I think it was only the first term, at the age of probably five. There were three classrooms in that little building, nearer the headmaster's house, and you gradually moved up. Mrs Carpenter was one of the teachers. And then you moved over into what we called the Big School - there was Miss Relf, who we were all terrified of. There was a variety of ages in the classes because you moved up with ability - if you weren't quite there, you might have to stay awhile.

A lot of girls stayed after they were eleven, only for another three years, there must have been other classes they went up to.

Primary Schools

Miss Relf ruled with a rod of iron. A word from her would have petrified you. I don't think she ever struck anybody. There was caning, but I don't think girls were ever caned. There was one man who was much feared for his caning, but I never got involved with him. The head was Mr Croucher - a lovely man - the organist at St Dunstan's. As it was a C of E school we had a lot to do with the church. The vicar came and spoke to us regularly - probably more than once a week... It was very difficult because it was during the war.

We had evacuees of course - extra people in, although some of the local people were evacuated out ... Mum made me have school dinners because of the rationing. I remember revolting stew with swede in it. I remember smuggling the swede out in my handkerchief, because we had to eat it. But every so often you got candied orange peel - I don't know how they did it as it needed sugar and oranges. But, every so often, a minute piece.

They were very strict. They kept you at it. I don't remember them bullying, or being frightened, but perhaps that was because I didn't find it all that difficult. I'd got good support at home - a very clever father... Lessons consisted of the basic three R's, I suppose. Loosely some geography and history, probably. A lot of religious education - a good bit of the morning on that. Singing lessons. Also handicrafts - simple, because there wasn't the material. I remember making raffia things. The boys also did the gardening - that little bit of garden outside the school. No science, but nature walks. Science really wouldn't have been any good to the local children as there was nothing for them to use it on. Most went into agriculture, although there were apprenticeships. Hutchison Roe took on a lot of apprentices for electricians, plumbers, the building trade.

Rodney Dann *was at the Primary School just after the war.*
The head was Bert Croucher, who later became head of Swattenden. I have vivid memories of Miss Relf, I remember

Primary Schools

her shaking me till my teeth rattled - I can't remember why, but it must have been something pretty bad... It was a nice little school. In those days it took all ages, four to fifteen, both sexes. I think there were between twenty and thirty children in a class, not so different from today. All the sport I remember was the BBC's 'Music and Movement' when we'd all leap around the classroom with our plimsolls on. But there was - I think instigated by Bill Jempson - a class of us came down in the evenings to the old grammar school gym, where we could climb the ropes and vault the horse. A little bit of football and cricket.

Mona Pittock *came to Cranbrook in 1949, when her husband, John, was appointed Headmaster of the Primary School. She remembers the children of the school, especially the senior girls.*

They were delightful, they really were; you see, John had half the girls; the boys had already gone to Swattenden at eleven, and John was left with the senior girls ... The school was very large, and there were very few facilities for these senior girls compared with the new Secondary Modern Schools they were building. They didn't seem to mind, and we tried very hard. The biggest facility was the HORSA hut; that was the hut built on the raising of the school leaving age from fourteen to fifteen, to relieve the pressure. One half of it was the Domestic Science Lab; now that was really good for the girls - they had a specialist teacher. The other half - when I look back it was really funny - but it was for assembly in the morning - it was used for music. It was used for PE on wet days, for dancing, drama, for anything, practically, and then at midday it was converted into a dining room for the girls. They were so good; they had to put up the trestle tables, you see, and then they had to go and carry all the containers from the old canteen, which was another hut. The juniors had their lunch in their classrooms on their desks, and the big girls carried all the stuff and looked after them, and I never heard a grumble, because I always went in and helped out because John found it difficult to get staff, they were taking jobs in the modern schools.

Conditions were hard - there was no hot water for them, it was really primitive. The juniors were very much, well, they were family, they were very much looked after by the older girls, there was a very nice atmosphere actually. Again - lavatories in the playground, which froze in the winter; conditions were hard - tortoise stoves - the old black stoves, with the big guards with a big rail round them... If John asked for anything, the reply always was, "Well, we won't spend any money because there's a new school coming," and it was eight years, those conditions lasted .

In the north west of the parish stands Colliers Green School, built by the generosity of Clement Cramp and the efforts of Canon William Bell, and opened in 1908. **Brigid Longley** *sent her children there in the 1960s.*

They went to Colliers Green, which had become quite popular. A wonderful lady called Mrs Head coped with the whole school with the aid of her friend whose name escapes me, and the year we sent Daniel they had just had proper loos put in. I think I wouldn't have sent him probably if they'd still got the earth closet... we're talking about 1960 or so... but still no electricity and in the afternoons in the winter, if it got very dark, it was impossible to go on with the lessons and they messed about or did a bit of gardening, I think... In those days there were about a dozen or more children, I think, who lived quite close to Colliers Green, because there were many more families working on the farms and so there were quite a few children lived around there. I think it was nearly as big as it is now, between 60 and 70, I think. Earlier, before the leaving age was raised, Miss Head had taught all the older ones. I think she was helped by the school leaving age still being only fourteen. Some of the older girls would help with teaching the younger ones.

SECONDARY SCHOOLS

'The Grammar', as Cranbrook School is widely known, is Cranbrook's oldest school, but it saw many changes in the 20th century, from small boys' public school to large co-educational selective school within the state system.

Sidney Barham *won a scholarship early in the 1900s.*

My father meant to have me educated, oh yes! He wanted me to have something better. That's why he kept me at the Grammar School, you see. I got the scholarship for a year and then it was renewed for five years. There was tuition - £3 and £5. They were the Dence scholarships. They were the moneys that had been allocated to a school that had been closed - Dence's School, and it had been sunk in the Grammar School to provide scholarships for elementary school boys.

Very few boys went to the Grammar School. There hadn't been hardly any, but the year I went in, several went in for it... And quite a lot of boys used to come over from Hawkhurst on their bicycles. They had county scholarships of some sort... One boy came all the way from Paddock Wood like that, by train.

In those days the afternoon school was from four to six, so there was a break in the middle of the day, that was to enable the boys to have some sport. These were day boys, you see, not boarders. It was originally a day boys' school, it was started for the boys of the town. But at the end of the 18th century or the beginning of the 19th century, one of the masters started boarding boys himself, so they could go to the school, you see. It was his idea, he got the money and all that, the boarding. And from that it began that there were boarders and boarders and boarders until there were more boarders than day boys.

Above : Class 3 in the Elementary School, probably 1920s.

Below : Sewing Class in the early days at Mary Sheafe School.

Secondary Schools

We were the outcasts as it were. There wasn't really any hostility, but they looked down on us a bit, because many of them were the sons of soldiers and sailors and goodness knows what. A good many of the boarders, their parents were abroad, in the consular service or in India or something. We were the day bugs. But we were the elite really, we were what the school was there for, the others were parasites, you might say.

Then, you see, there were private schools for girls in the town. There was the Miss Huntley School in the High Street, that was very aristocratic, very nice they were, very prim and proper. Then there was another little school, Miss Carly's. They were also high and mighty, but not quite so high and mighty. There had been one or two Dame Schools in Cranbrook, but they were dead by this time.

Fifty years later, **Peter Jempson** *followed in Sidney Barham's footsteps as a day boy.*

I think we counted as a sort of minor Public School because the headmaster was on the Headmasters' Conference. We used to go and play at the Public Schools' hockey tournament at Oxford, so that was a sort of cachet, I suppose.

Certainly we were looked down on by some of the boarders... As you went up the school and showed you were intellectually and games-wise as good as they were, things evened out a bit. I ended up quite enjoying it there.

The uniform was sacrosanct. If you went into the town, you were supposed to 'cap'. That is, you were supposed to raise your finger to your brow as if you were touching the peak of your cap - you didn't have caps - you had to make the gesture to members of staff and their wives if you met them in the town. And you weren't supposed to speak to your parents if they were out in the town at the same time as you were.

I think there were three or four of my contemporaries went to Cambridge, there may have been more at Oxford at the time. Quite a lot of people used to go into business and the professions. In fact quite a lot of day boys left at the end of the fifth year and pursued suitable careers somewhere else. There wasn't quite the mad dash to go for a degree in those days.

After teaching at Mary Sheafe School, **Mona Pittock** *moved to 'the Grammar' in 1968. She remembers being a woman in a male staff-room, and the changes which came in the early '70s*

I knew several of the staff before I went there; they did accept me very well indeed. They had this terrible old Staff Room with the holly tree growing up through the floor. I was never made to feel unwelcome as I had done during the war at an all boys school. The boys were good too. I mean, they tried it on a bit, but they soon learned not to.

Then Peter Rowe *(Headmaster 1970-81)* came, and I think he more or less - I won't say 'smuggled', it's the wrong word, but they allowed a few sixth form girls in. It changed the school quite a lot ... There were many boys I didn't even know their Christian names because we had always called them by their surnames, and then suddenly I thought: "Well, you can't call a girl Mary and then turn round and say 'Smith, do so and so' ". So I started learning the names of the boys. I think it made for a more informal atmosphere.

I think the transformation went very well indeed... You expect an explosion and it didn't happen . It all went, I thought, rather quietly. I remember one form I had was very competitive, the boys, and they were a very good form. They were very resentful because the girls beat them to answering the questions every time, and you would see this look of surprise on their faces: "Good heavens, we've got to compete with this!" And in that way I think it did good.

The Education Act of 1945 required that all children should transfer to a Secondary School at the age of eleven. In Cranbrook, the only secondary school was Cranbrook School, but a new boys' school was soon set up at Swattenden. **Rodney Dann** *was a pupil there in the early days.*

Mr. Croucher was head there by that time. Education consisted of the three 'R's, but we were there to do bee keeping, pig keeping, make ladders - really a rural industry education more than it should have been, with good Maths and English.

(As well as agriculture) ...the other major industry was the dolly factory at Hawkhurst - the wood turning. It employed quite a lot of people, probably the second major labour user

At thirteen you could take exams for the tech. By the time I was thirteen I'd already started working, holidays and weekends, for pocket money and the line I wanted was agriculture and horticulture. Swattenden was great for that. Trevor Thomas, the gardening master, Pat Field, Mr Harding (Rural Studies), and the woodwork and metalwork were useful.

Girls had to wait longer for their own secondary school. It came in 1958, with the founding of Mary Sheafe School. **Monica Camburn** *was the first teacher to be appointed there.*

Girls all through the '50s had had to continue either at Hawkhurst or at Cranbrook Primary as senior girls, along with the infants and junior children who were there. So that when we started Mary Sheafe, it was quite a... almost a terrifying

Secondary Schools

experience for the girls. I can remember the first day of term... We saw all these girls, about 300 to 350 of them, standing in quite nervous groups. And the groups were the villages the children had come from, not their own peer groups, but all the children from Frittenden together, all the children from Kilndown together, and so on.

The school seemed quite a happy school. Quiet, well disciplined ... and we at the start were a small staff and we were very friendly and a very well-knit staff really, in a way that you can only have when the staff isn't too large.

I remember that my own first class was a 3B. It was about the largest class there was. I seem to remember there were 38 of them and people looked in horror and raised their hands in horror at this. But as I had taught in south-east London they didn't really present any problems to me.

Mona Pittock transferred to Mary Sheafe from the Primary School at the same time as many of the senior girls (11-to 15-year-olds).

(At the Primary School) the girls seemed very happy; I still see a lot of them, and some of them are grandmothers, and I think they had a great affection for it , because I know I took them up once or twice while the Sheafe was being built and tried to sell it to them, saying, "This is your new school", but their eyes didn't light up at all. They didn't like the idea of change... of course it was a complete contrast, with its shiny corridors and labs and beautiful assembly hall and so forth, it was really very nice. They hadn't done a language before, and hadn't had science labs. No, they were exciting days, because there was so much change.

In 1970, Swattenden and Mary Sheafe were combined to form

a single school on the site of Mary Sheafe. It was called Angley School. Monica Camburn describes the preparations for the change.

A series of meetings was held with representatives from the staff of Mary Sheafe and the staff of Swattenden, and head teachers and representatives from the Local Education Authority... We realised that Swattenden and Mary Sheafe were going to be put together. I remember very clearly that the feeling of the staff of both schools was that this should happen by children coming in at eleven from all the primary schools which contribute nowadays to Angley School, and the school building up from there, particularly as there were going to be new buildings which hadn't been started at that stage. However, despite anything that was said, it was decided in the end that the authorities wished to amalgamate the schools immediately... We would have to use both school buildings, Mary Sheafe and Swattenden, a fair distance apart, which we did use a great deal for the first two years.

Michael Head, the headmaster, had been appointed a year earlier, but it was quite interesting initiating change, in that we were taking in a comprehensive intake for two years, then the selected ones were transferring to Cranbrook, but, looking back, and perhaps being wise after the event, it could have been managed a bit better if the two contributory schools had prepared the ground a bit. We went up to 1300 fairly quickly, when we were still working with the junior school at Swattenden, because the builders went bust, so the building of the school on the Angley site was much delayed. So Angley survived; the first two or three years were a little exciting at times, but it settled down and, I think, became a good school.

Aerial view of Cranbrook School, probably between the Wars.

MEDICINE

Probably few things changed more in the 20th century than the treatment available if you were ill or injured.

Treatment for a bad foot, 1900-style, described by **Charles Evernden.**

I was only about five then I suppose, in those days we were hard up you know, there was six of us in the family, and one man's wages wasn't much. We used to get hold of second-hand shoes sometimes, you know, to fit us, and whether they were too big or not you had to wear them. I had a nail right in the ball of my foot, and I'd just started school then, and I was laid up for weeks with this. The treatment was boiled linseed, linseed poultices. Linseed was boiled and put on hot, you know. I know I had that put on twice a day for weeks and weeks, that came up in a great big lump there... That was swollen up till it burst... But that was the main sort of treatment - poultices, you know. If you got pneumonia, well, you was good as finished...

A few years later, Charles Evernden had a polyp removed at Maidstone Hospital.

When I was young I had a polypus in my nose, that's a sort of growth that grows at the back of your nose.... I pushbiked to Maidstone, that's fourteen miles, went in this room, nearly dark, you know, and they'd only got little lamps. That was just before the First World War. There was about three doctors working in this room, you had an outpatients' department, you see. He put this thing over his head, you know, with a reflecting mirror with a hole in the middle of it, and I had to hold the kidney basin up under my nose, and he hooked my nose up and stuck a swab in there, and then he got these forceps and he took about seven or eight pieces out of the back of my nose sort of business, gristle, broke off gristle, till I couldn't stand any more, and I pushed him away. Cor, they'd make a fuss these days, wouldn't they! They said go out there and wash, there was only a tap out there. I had to wash it and the blood was running down my face.

It bled to the afternoon. I pushbiked home riding one hand holding the handkerchief there squeezing the blood out as I went home, you see. Cor dear, that was crude , that was.

Charles Forward *remembers going into hospital as a child.*

Now I remember when I was about five years old I had to go to Maidstone Hospital to have my tonsils and adenoids removed. We went up with the old horse bus and in those days you just sat on the nurse's knee. I suppose they numbed it somehow and they just yanked it out on the nurse's knee. And you went back into a recovery room where it was kids all crying and various states all round. They didn't put you under, and you didn't stay long in hospital. But they didn't take them out clean because I had mine out a second time when I was 21. They told me then that they take them out roots and all now. They used to cut them off, in some cases it was like pruning a rose tree, the doctor told me, and they grew stronger than ever afterwards.

Brigid Longley *was the daughter of a dentist in the days before the National Health Service.*

We had panel patients who paid (do you know, I'm not sure how the panel worked) but they'd obviously paid into something, probably one of the old societies. When I first started work, for instance, I had to pay fourpence a week to Mrs Bottle in the sweet shop for my Ancient Foresters stamp which I had to have. A lot of people had no treatment, and a lot of people wouldn't have thought of coming at all. I don't remember any horror stories of people who pulled out teeth for twopence or something, which went on a bit before that.

Medicine

She remembers the 'Infant Welfare'.

One thing that I remember going back to my childhood was the Infant Welfare in Cranbrook where my mother helped for seventeen years. All the mothers brought their babies, or most of them, and they were weighed and they could get free medical attention there if it was needed. And that happened in the Bull Room; we used to go up the iron staircase to the Bull Room. If there was a child born with a club foot or a hare lip or something, everybody got together to raise money for the operation because otherwise that child would not have had any help at all.

Dr John Hooper, *who came to Cranbrook in 1958, looks back to general practice in the early days of the NHS.*

I had known nothing else, and that I think was an advantage. The older members of the profession here had had tremendous changes thrust upon them, and some of it they felt was not fair; it was much easier for younger people to enter general practice, because the buying and selling of practices had been abolished in 1948. So I was able to take on a practice single handed. It was a deliberate choice not to go into partnership, I felt that the Health Service had not really settled down to give partnerships a happy future together. I had sufficient work to do, perhaps more than sufficient. My predecessor, who was a very good doctor, died very suddenly, and his notes gave me that information, that he was very good. I was taking on a very good practice and didn't need to try and expand it. We didn't really have time off and it didn't really seem to matter in those days. It wasn't expected in hospital practice, for junior appointments, there really was no time off.

Doctors had much more freedom, as Doctor Hooper recalls.

We had an amazing amount of professional freedom at that

stage; one was on trust, and I think that did seem to work satisfactorily. There was no restriction on referrals at all. I could refer to Pembury, Tunbridge Wells, Maidstone, Hastings or Ashford, and because I had done my training in London, I knew consultants at Guy's Hospital and St Mary's Hospital and still referred quite a large percentage to London. I was free to refer patients much more widely than is available now or in the 1990s.

If one wanted a patient seen quickly, that was possible. It was quite in order to phone up the consultant, present your problem to him or her, and that patient would be seen immediately, and if I referred a patient to a clinic at Guy's Hospital, they would be seen by a consultant that day. The clinics at Guy's were open-ended; one was expected to respect this, but nevertheless it was available, and if you used it with discretion, it was extremely valuable both to the doctor and to the patient.

Dr Hooper describes the changes that happened in his practice during his time.

It did tend to expand, probably only because the numbers in the neighbourhood grew gradually, and it did expand to a point where, after about twenty years, for a spell I didn't take on any new patients, because to do so would overburden this practice. This wasn't an easy thing to do. And one had to be very strict that it was absolute, that we didn't pick and choose who we took, that would have been quite unfair. I think I had a normal mix of patients, but a younger doctor, if he has his own family, tends to grow up and grow old with you. I had had more hospital experience in children's departments, both at Guy's and at St Mary's and at one time wondered about working only in pediatrics, but in the end the choice to go into general practice seemed to suit our needs, and we did aim to secure a practice which had a school.

Medicine

I inherited Benenden School from my predecessor and it amounted to about 20% of the practice, and it was a very good interest for us. One's first responsibility was the child, but the parents had sent their children to a private school, and of course one liaised properly with them and their own doctors at home, but one also had a responsibility to the school, particularly on matters of public health. That was part of one's responsibility as a medical officer to a school, and a very interesting one. Hard work when there was an epidemic, certainly!

Changes in the health of the people of Cranbrook.

There were major changes with regard to home births. A practice of normal size could expect to have about thirty births a year, and in the 1960s and '70s at least half of these were at home, simply because the hospitals couldn't provide beds for everybody. In my experience mothers did very well at home and we were fortunate never to run into any serious difficulties, but as the facilities at Pembury increased and the equipment to make births safer also increased, that was gradually phased out.

Overall, there have been some significant improvements in the health of the people of Cranbrook. Better housing, better nutrition, better hygiene all have played a big part. Antibiotics and vaccines have also played a big part, and morbidity has diminished over these years. Waste disposal has been enormously improved, the sewage system has increased gradually over the years, and food hygiene has improved...at the point of sale, but not always within the domestic community!

Dr Hooper expresses his views on the work of a GP.

In general practice, you see that person in their family or in their normal way of life, and that is extremely helpful. When you see a person in a hospital bed there's an awful lot missing in your knowledge . So, yes, the observation of the pattern of life, and the changes in the person that you observe over the years should be extremely valuable in assisting in diagnosis, which is one's main role as a general practitioner. You call yourself a general practitioner, you're not concerned just with part of them, so, of course, it must be holistic medicine. One may not see them frequently in the surgery, but in a small town, you see them in other roles, on a cricket field or in church. What's that person looking in that window for? It's part of the fascination.

Only when I left it did I realize what an enormous burden one was shouldering, and the relief of leaving it came as a surprise, and now I have tremendous respect for the stress that my colleagues accept as their normal way of life. I had the feeling that I had been very well trained, and if anybody was able to accept the responsibility I should be amongst them.

SHOPS

Evernden's, the celebrated Stone Street hardware store, had long been run by **Charles Evernden,** *and his grandfather and father before him, as a saddler's until he converted it after the Second World War.*

When I was a boy, my grandfather kept four skilled saddlers on, you know, up to 1914 - then an odd man to collect the work and deliver it. And a woman in the shop to do book keeping and that sort of thing. In those days shops weren't like they are now. I mean the shop - the selling part - was so small really: it was a workshop and shop combined - we used to have a workbench and all in the shop. Had two counters, one behind the other where you worked at - and that was like that till after,

Shops

well, the 1920s, I suppose, before we did away with that...

We employed one or two saddlers after the First World War when I was in it. But it was only through war wounds that brought me into the trade: I should never have been a saddler if it hadn't been for a war wound. I got knocked about, so I was more or less an invalid for several years, and I learnt the trade in the '20s... All the shops used to have their own scents in those days. If you went into a shop in the old days, you knew what it was because of this. You could go in with your eyes shut. You knew what sort of shop you was in. I still think the saddler's shop was the best scent of the lot...You get different leathers - they've all got that little different scent. Then blended with the Stockholm Tar. Stockholm Tar and leather smell, they go together, see.

And of course the shop was always hanging, all the ceiling, rows and rows of hemp, ropes and lines of all sizes, you know. Everything was - then the fashion came, oh, everybody must keep their ceilings clean, have them white painted and the rest of it, you know. We kept our brushes and brooms hanging up on them. It came back into fashion again, just the same...

You could always tell a saddler in the old days because he had all these big cuts on his little fingers, you see. Sometimes they got so bad, on some jobs, especially long boots sort of thing, heavy like that. Keep pulling hard, and hard harness, breechings and that. The thread would cut into your fingers, you see. Used to put finger stools on like, you know. No tip on them, you see - just made a rough finger stool round there. Save your fingers. Otherwise you've got to make the wax hot, put it in the gas jet, melt it, let it run into the cracks and fill them up, you see... About the best remedy there was, I think. Harden your finger edges... form a harder skin on it afterwards, see...

Established 1832.

C. I. EVERNDEN,
Saddler & Harness Maker,
CRANBROOK.

Attends Benenden every Monday & Thursday
from 3 to 8 p.m.
(ADJOINING MR. MALPASS, BLACKSMITH.)

All Orders promptly executed.

ALSO KEEPS A LARGE STOCK OF
Brushes, Brooms and Mops, Ropes, Lines and Twines for Farm, Stable, House or Garden.

Advertisement for Samuel Evernden, saddler, 1915.

John Hart, proprietor, in front of Everndens shortly before closure in August 2000.

Shops

The shops in general, I mean before the First World War, well, they never thought of closing much before ten o'clock at night - I mean Saturday nights, I mean. *(Elsewhere Mr Evernden said that the saddler's used to be open from 8 am to 6 pm on weekdays.)* Never worked Sundays: nobody did. Not in those days. Gracious me, they wouldn't think of working Sundays... Now they work Sundays and Good Friday and all, don't they? Open shops and all. Disgraceful, I think it is...

They only used to charge 6d an hour for labour you know, in those days you know, up to the first world war, and they never paid their bills, you know, farmers. Farmers were notorious for that. Well, even the Earl of Cranbrook... he only used to pay once in six months, and sometimes he'd got twelve, you see, depending on the steward, you see, whoever it was, you see. But I mean you could go several years sometimes before you got your money. Farmers, some of the devils wouldn't pay, they didn't want to. I know my father one day, he got hold of one old farmer by the beard, you know, and he said if you don't pay me, I'll pay you... I suppose they were hard up too. I don't know, times were difficult for everybody, weren't they?

When **Ted Ratcliff's** *father married in 1903, he moved from Goudhurst to Cranbrook and took over the butcher's shop in what is now Rovi. Ted joined the business in 1925 and finally closed it down in 1973.*

The shop which is Rovi now, that was our sitting room. Where The Country House is, that was the shop... At the back, originally there was the slaughterhouse, and the tack room where we had horses, stables; and there was the wood shed; an outside toilet. The garden came right to the boundary of Cranbrook School.

The slaughterhouse was used until 1940 - the beginning of the

Shops

war. That was all stopped: rationing came in, meat rationing carried on till 1953-54 - then slaughterhouses had to be very much more up to date, and it wasn't used as a slaughterhouse any more. We bought our meat 'off the hook'...

When we first started, we used to go round the area, markets and also from farmers. We used to buy live cattle. We also had ground, about thirty acres, which we used to graze: Wheatfield Way, Wheatfield Drive, Oatfield Close - all built on now. We were butchers and graziers... Cattle we used to bring in to graze - not many sheep. Pigs we used to buy locally, more or less every fortnight, from different markets around - Goudhurst, Staplehurst, Paddock Wood - up to the Second World War. We used to walk *(the cattle)* for miles, from Goudhurst, Staplehurst, even from Paddock Wood - that's the only way you could do it. Men called drovers used to drive these cattle for people from the markets...

You know Oatfield Drive, that was one entrance to one of the fields, and the other one was opposite to Angley School itself - a little pathway down. We also had an exit into Bank Street: we would bring two or three cattle at a time *(down High Street)*, as we wanted them. It was quite a usual thing in those days: nobody thought anything of it at all. Cattle had to be walked around like that...

(The age for slaughter was) as a rule round about two and a half to three years. We used to look at their mouth and see if they'd got six teeth, and that was OK. If they'd got a full mouth, you knew they were getting older, and the meat would be too tough. Four to six teeth: four teeth is two years, six teeth is three years. You knew whether they'd got a good back, a nice straight back - we used to feel them under their coats. Look at it and see its front, you would see what its crop-end, its chest was like. It sounds silly, but there is an art...

Shops

We were distributing two and a half bullocks a week - sometimes we would kill two a week, sometimes three. In the winter time, you would have five or six pigs: pork wasn't very popular in the summer time. We got a terrific amount of Canterbury Lamb from New Zealand: we would sell twenty to thirty lambs a week. They came down in lorries. We never touched bacon at all, or game - we had no game licence...

(For disposal) we used to have a dung cart, that was quite near the shed at the back. We used to take it up to Hancocks Farm at Tilsden twice a week and he used to put it on his dung mixin. Sheppey Glue came round twice a week, until recent years when they only came once a week - I believe they still go to Mr Wilkes - and they would buy all the bones. The hides: a firm from Tonbridge used to come down on a Tuesday morning and take the hides and all the skins. A firm named Staggs... *(The photo on page 91 shows meat hanging all the way across the Ratcliffs' shop, dining room and yard door.)* That was customary in those days. You put it out in the morning and fetched it in the evening. Dirt and dust didn't matter - you were tough in those days...

You used to start at six o'clock in the morning and the shop was opened at seven o'clock. I would go into breakfast at half past eight. Then go round the Cranbrook area for orders, go back and deliver them the same day, in time for lunch - on a bicycle. We closed at seven o'clock in the evenings. We used to go up to nine o'clock on a Friday night, getting the orders ready. In the summer time, when we didn't have much refrigeration, we used to start at three o'clock on a Saturday morning...

That was in the days of bicycles. We had a horse to start off with: I didn't do much with the horse because I was too young. Eventually we sold the last horse and bought a van: 1925... When I had the van, I used to go out as much as three times

Stone Street shops

91

Shops

every day - all round Benenden, nearly into Goudhurst, out to Rounds Green by Blantyre House, parts of Sissinghurst, parts of Golford. That was three days a week.

Eileen Woodcock, *with her sister*, **Doreen Rivers**, *worked in the International Stores, first in Stone Street and then when it transferred to High Street at the beginning of the 1960s.*

I was seventeen when I went there - that was '41. There were only half a dozen of us worked there then, and the lads had to go off into the army and that just left the girls to do the work.

Everything came in big bags. Butter was 70 lb. boxes, plus the weight of the boxes, which were wooden. And everything was loose, nothing was come in pre-packed. Sugar, soap flakes - oh, that was the worst thing! Have you ever tried to shovel soap flakes into a bag? Soda. Well, everything. You bagged it up beforehand, when we weren't serving, and things like that. You had different coloured bags, but it just depends what you got at that time - you had what you could get. When you did up the orders for people, and there weren't no boxes in those days to do them up, so we used to tie them up in parcels, in brown paper parcels, with a bit of string all round. There was all the orders - funny shaped parcels. Soap, scrubbing soap, came in a yard length, like that, which you cut with a piece of string into better sized soap...

Rationing in wartime, so there wasn't as much as there is now. There was a few things which you could get which weren't rationed, but not a lot. And when it came to doing the butter, cheese, bacon - all the things that were rationed - in ounces and two ounces! Ounce and a half of cheese: you got to cut that exactly - you didn't dare give them a bit overweight or underweight, so if you cut off a bit that was a bit too big, you got to slice a tiny bit off, and try to put it on to something else.

The butter and marge had to be knocked up with butter pats. We'd do two ounces and four ounces when we got the spare time. When people came in for their rations, you knew what they got to have, you knew they was coming in. They came in each week: you could get it all ready for them. Cake, there wasn't enough cake to go round - one week we did them for the orders and the next week it was for the counter, the people that came in... Fruit cake or Madeira, you had to cut. In those days it used to come in about six or seven pound slabs - and you had to put them on the scales, in half an ounce, work it all out in your head. There were no machines to do it. These days they've just got these calculators. You had the balance scales, like the kitchen scales... Just as you went in the door there was the cash desk, then the mahogany counter, with groceries on it.

And on the left hand side there was the Provisions, with the marble *(counter)*... Just inside the door there was a little cash desk. When we served the customers we had a - like a raffle ticket. Then you added up what the customer - tear off the ticket, then they would take the ticket to the cash desk, then she *(the cashier)* would take the money...

We did a lot of orders. We had to go out on a pushbike and collect orders from customers... Then we had a van which we shared with Tenterden branch - so many days at Tenterden, and so many at Cranbrook... Later on we had another one, which we had to share with Hawkhurst as well. On a Thursday - this was later on - we were doing a hundred orders, deliveries, on a Thursday. Whereas when I started, I don't suppose we did more than a hundred a week, which was the difference. We used to go to Goudhurst, Staplehurst, Frittenden, Sissinghurst - quite a round - Benenden. I think the worst one was going out into Benenden forest, into Hemsted forest - used to go right out in the middle there. You'd get so far, then you'd have to get out and walk. When the planes were going over the top of you, it

*Milk and coal deliveries
at the beginning of the 20th century.*

wasn't much fun. That order was posted in. Local customers, you'd get them in those days, they used to ring up: "I want half a pound of rashers. Cut them for - rind this. Bring them up as soon as possible..." I want it now, you know. And you'd be expected to do it and take it straight away. That's how it was in those days.

There was a lot of grocers in Cranbrook. There was the World Stores, where Miles is now. There was Allen's at the top of The Hill. There was Chittenden's opposite, which is now Ina Monk's. There was Farren's, which is now the dry cleaners. There was Rumens', was a grocers, on the corner. There was the Co-op, that started up just before the war. They were all competing with each other. There was as many grocers as there was pubs then.

THE HAND LAUNDRY

Maria Dann *began to work for the Court family's hand laundry in Tippens Close in the 1920s, and continued there until Miss Court's death and the closing of the laundry in the early 1970s.*

I went there, I think I must have been about sixteen. First of all, I think my mother was working there, and she didn't want me to go into service yet because she said I could help at home a bit: and so in the end I went up there. The first thing I always remember, I started on ironing the serviettes; oh, they were lovely, they had the lovely damask ones in those days. I used to do those mostly - anything plain like that - for a start. I think I must have been born to it, because I love ironing. I just went on like that...

The Hand Laundry

This started before this Miss Court took it on. Her aunt had it before her, and she was a laundrymaid down at Angley House in Tomlin's time... In the first place, what is Rammell House now, it was Neves that had it, and they owned all places. And it was on understanding that the laundry was done there, and we did theirs. And I remember - you know the old-fashioned cotton nighties, with frills: well, Miss Fanny Neve and Mrs Neve wore those, and one of the cooks, she did. She was a little old-fashioned body. I remember one woman, she used to iron: she said, "Is this the lady's, or the cook's?" If it was the cook's, it didn't get so well ironed - she didn't trouble over her! Still, it was done. She was a good ironer. We used to laugh about it.

In the ironing room there was a back door at the top end. The washing was done there. When I first went there, there was what was called a Dolly tub. Mr Court used to wash the sheets, and then they were just put through a rubber wringer that was fixed on this tub. Sheets and big bath towels, I think, he did. There was another tub against the far wall, and that was for shirts and things. It was a wooden tub, and you had a board down it and a scrubbing brush, and you scrubbed collars and cuffs, and just washed where it was necessary. I didn't do much washing - that wasn't up my street. I did hanging out...

(The water was heated) in an old copper, brick-built, in the corner. That was boiling there. Then we had another - we had two tubs and this Dolly tub. Of course eventually we went to twin tub. Mr Court was disgusted. He said, "You can't call it a Hand Laundry any more." But, any rate, it was a great relief to do that. But that was latter part, about ten years, I suppose...

(For drying,) in the garden, we had lines: but chiefly up in that estate - we had a field at the top, I should think it would come about opposite the ambulance station. We had lines up there. The fields belonged to Oaklands *(now Rammell House)*, you

see. Miss Court had to pay a shilling a year to be able to do that. At the same time that field was let for animals. One time they had bullocks up there - I didn't like them at all. They used to get in the clothes. One of them got their horns through a sheet, a practically new sheet. Oh, there was a fuss. I think Miss Court must have mended it, 'cos she wouldn't have sent it back as it was. But, anyrate, she had to replace that. It was Mrs Levett it belonged to, and of course she was most upset about that. It was a nuisance. And in the winter time, when it was icy and snow - I've been up there lots of time. You'd just go round beating your hands, keeping warm. But that was the only way, and often we didn't get them dry. In these days you wouldn't accept it. With bath towels, when you did get them dry, they didn't smell nice. That was the trouble then, drying. Of course it did dry in the laundry, but not as well, when you've got big sheets. We used to have lines all across and hang out - oh, it was a job.

(The irons, of varying sizes, were heated on stoves.) You've seen that little stove up there: well, those. I've still got one... I wish, in a way, I hadn't given all the little polishing irons. That's one of them - it's nice... We had big eight-pound ones there, that we did have, and they used to - the handles got worn and broke and several were thrown out. That one I sometimes use now, if I want to do something and don't want to bother with the electric. I stand it on the stove and it gets hot, and I do little odd bits if I want something.... Yes, they're good. Yes, there were seven or eight on that stove: then we could get one in the front - nine; and little one or two on the top, and I think the back - yes, at the back we could get two. That stove that's up there *(at the museum)*, I can remember Miss Court having that, and Hutchison Roe it came from. When the chap came to put it up, he couldn't see how it went, and I helped him put it together - I always felt cocky over that...

(To fuel it,) Mr Court used to fetch coke when he was able

The Hand Laundry

from the gasworks *(on The Hill)*. And in those days you'd get a hundredweight of coke - in those days you'd get two bags - you'd get more than a hundredweight, because they used to get such a lot there. It was tipped out in the laundry, in the chimney corner. That's where we kept it then. Then when he couldn't - well, when he wasn't there - Miss Court and I used to go. Or Mr Woodcock worked, 'cos he worked at the gasworks for years, and he used to bring it up. When he couldn't, we'd been down and fetched it, more than once. Well, I couldn't now, but we did go. He had a hand cart to fetch that on - he had this hand cart, and used to fetch the laundry from up the town. We had hampers there and people used those, and we had from the Clarks at the Abbey, that were then, Tutts from higher up the High Street. Several people - I can't remember them all - in the town, that Miss Court did for. It was sheets and towels chiefly, sheets and pillows and that kind of thing.

We had a mangle there, a wooden mangle - sheets, we used to have to fold the sheets, and they always went right through the mangle. I remember a traveller came, and he was right too - we thought he was silly - and he said, "Of course you know what you are doing. You're just mangling the creases in the sheets." Which, of course, we were. We always had to iron them, but the idea was to mangle them to help with the ironing, but it really didn't because we did get them nice and dry - they were brought down and folded . But when they were left in a heap, they were much easier to do that way, straightaway. But they were always mangled in those days. When I think about it, my mother did just the same - we used to have a mangle there to mangle clothes, but it did mangle the creases in really...

Rinsing, we had from this copper there was a big sink at the side. Miss Court had what was called a draining board, and they were fished out of the copper and on to the draining board, so that as much water as possible went back in the copper. And then we had a big bath of water in the sink - we used to rinse in that. That was a tub and not a bath, and that had a wooden wringer on the end and you had to wring them out of that. Of course, when the blessed wringers got a bit worn, it didn't dry as much as it ought to do. That was a nuisance. That's how you had to go on...

So we, you know, it just gradually went with people dying and people moving away. Miss Court was getting older and it just wasn't worth it. But we did have quite a lot there, and of course during the beginning of the war, I don't know if you remember we had soldiers camped up in the field here then - there was no building - and the boys used to come down with their officers' laundry. Would we do it, would we help them? Till the officers found out what they were doing - they got into trouble! But we used to do those, and wash and mend the socks and things. It was nice to be able to. That's how we went on.

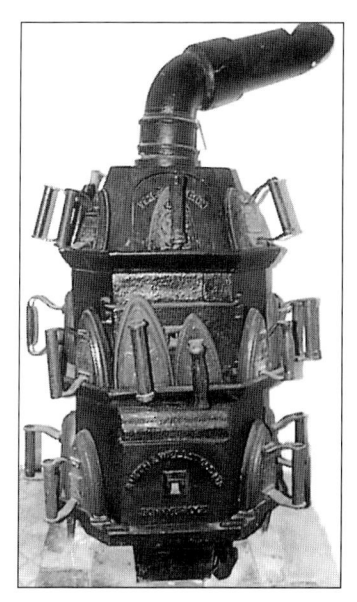

Flat Iron heating stove used by Miss Court until 1970. Now in Cranbrook Museum.

SOME 'CHARACTERS'

We have few oral descriptions of individual Cranbrookians in the first half of the century. But **'Sonny' Hall** *memorably described the formidable Billy Winch (1853-1931), auctioneer, brewer, great landowner - widely referred to as "uncrowned king of Cranbrook".*

Mr Billy Winch, senior partner in Winch and Sons, with two brothers, but he was the dominating character of the three. Pickwickian in appearance: dressed with top hat, sideboards, cravat, frock coat, check breeches, white canvas gaiters buttoned up and black boots. In his left hand he carried a book and an auctioneer's gavel, and in the other his stick - a long one nearly as high as his shoulder and his thumb over the top in a Y-piece - and he'd walk majestically up the middle of the road and woe betide anyone who rang a bell or blew a hooter - he was Mr Winch, going to the office. There was one man, though, who used to like to come behind him, John Borrie from Biddenden: he used to shout "Get out of the way, you silly old bugger, you'll get run over in a minute!"

Probably no other leading local figure was as well known as Billy Winch until the far more lovable Bill Jempson half a century later. But there were 'characters' of quite another type, of which progress of some sort seems largely to have deprived Cranbrook by the end of the millennium. For an alert Cranbrook schoolboy like **Garry Blanch** *in the 1950s, the little town was full of them.*

One of them was Mr Curl, who used to live up by the allotments. And he used to come around selling paraffin, with an old push-cart. And he used to be out till 10, 11 or 12 o'clock at night, selling paraffin. You'd get a knock on your

Some 'Characters'

door, and he would come around asking if you wanted any paraffin. He was a great character and he'd come out with all these sayings. And he'd come up to you and say, "Till bum feather." And you'd say, "What are you on about, then?" And he'd say, "A little bit warmer in the weather." Then he'd say, "You don't want to go up to that Ball Field 'cos I've just seen a lion up there." And you'd say, "I don't believe you." And he'd say, "Yes, a dandelion.".. He was always about on the street corners, selling his paraffin.

Another one was the old chimney sweep called Slasher, who used to live in a row of terraced cottages which were pulled down in the '50s where Circle C *(Alldays)* now stands. Slasher was a chimney sweep and he used to have an old pram and all his equipment in there, and he used to push it all round Cranbrook and sweep people's chimneys... He was another one who was always standing on the street corner, and when we were kids we were fascinated by him 'cos he used to come out with all these stories. When the new post office was being built, they dug a big hole to put the boilers and that in. And we were talking to him one day and he said, "I'm standing here, you know, 'cos old Ben Farrer the policeman he said 'I want you to stop here, George, and look after that hole there, and make sure no-one takes it,' he said. So I'm standing here because I don't want no-one to take that hole away."

Then there was Sniffer Eaves. The Eaves family used to live in a house opposite the Duke of York - no longer there - a row of cottages which were a lean-to along the wall there. There must have been half a dozen of these cottages. Sniffer lived there with his brother Bumble, and the other one was called Shrimp. Sniffer had a big hump on his back and he used to work for Spicers in Stone Street, which is now the cafe, Soho South. He used to deliver all the veg. in his little push cart. We used to call him names, and everything, and he used to chase us all over the show. He couldn't run, and he used to chase us and call us

Some 'Characters'

all the names under the sun...

Sam Dann many people will remember because he died recently. He was the sexton and he used to look after Cranbrook churchyard and help with the grave digging at the cemetery.

When I was young, we used to live in the caretaker's cottage. My grandmother always said that Father Time used to come down at night and cut the grass, so we used to spend a lot of time looking out the window at night trying to see him coming down and cutting the grass. We used to say, "We can't see any grass cut." She would say, "Well, you go round behind the church and you'll see where it's cut." And we used to go round there and see old Sam and he'd say, "Yeah, he come down last night. Helps me out, and I don't have to do so much work, see." We always wondered why he was sitting in the churchyard drinking cups of tea - if someone came to cut the grass for him, he didn't need to do so much.

*Sam Dann,
Gravedigger,
on retirement at
the age of 86.*

*Father Time.
One of his rare
descents.*

BILL JEMPSON
Councillor Extraordinary

For much of the second half of the century, the best known figure in the running of Cranbrook's affairs was Bill Jempson, who was for many years a member of the Parish Council, the Rural District Council, later the Tunbridge Wells Borough Council, and the Kent County Council. **Peter Jempson** *describes how his father became involved in local government.*

He was born at Mountfield in 1908, I think, went to the local primary school, which he left at thirteen... Then he met my mother and they married in 1934 at Providence Chapel in Cranbrook. At some point he learned hairdressing and the two of them ran the double-fronted shop next door to the fishmonger's in the High Street, which was called the Tudor Saloons. And he worked doing men's hair cutting on one side and my mother did ladies' hairdressing on the other. His war effort was fire watching, and in addition to having the saloon he also cut the hair of the pupils in the boarding houses at Cranbrook School.

Then, I think, because he came into contact with a lot of people and realised the Parish Council was largely dominated by the landed gentry, gentlemen farmers, and well-to-do businessmen, he thought they were out of touch with the people, and he formed a Ratepayers' Association... and he was co-opted onto the Parish Council in 1944. He got to know people through his trade, his hairdressing. He was always looking out to see what was going on in the High Street, and people's ears were at severe risk.

He had none of the advantages that I've had, but he became a very skilled communicator. And he was also a very good listener, of course, which is one of the other prerequisites of a councillor... In 1946 he stood for the Rural District Council and got on. And I think that was the same year as he stood as an Independent for Parliament. Cranbrook was in the Ashford Division in those days, and he learned that Bill Deedes was being put up by the Conservatives and wasn't going to be opposed by anybody, and he felt it was an affront to democracy if somebody was going to be returned unopposed, so he stood. He got a few votes, but he didn't get in to beat Bill Deedes, of course, who was very well known. But I remember going along - it was in the days when the hustings were the normal thing - and my father challenged Bill Deedes to a debate, and it was held in the Drill Hall in Causton Road. I remember going along, and there were Bill Deedes and my father, you know, stating their policies or points of view.

Before long they made him Chairman of the Rural District Council; that was Cranbrook and surrounding parishes - Goudhurst and Kilndown at the one end round to Sandhurst and Benenden, Iden Green, Frittenden.

Peter Jempson goes on to describe Bill's interest in housing and education

Basically he stood because thought ordinary people ought to be listened to. His first priority was to be available. In fact, when I was growing up there was a steady stream of phone calls and people who walked round to see him in the evening... But one of the things that needed doing immediately after the war, where we had had about seven years of very little building and only bomb damage repair under licence, was to build houses for the forces who were being demobbed. And that's when all the major estates in the area were developed... That was the main achievement; there was a constant stream of people returning from the war, meeting up with wives and families who had been living perhaps with in-laws for security and moral support. We had a prefab estate called the Orchard Estate which was behind where Orchard Way is now, and of course that was a half-way house, but a lot of people were not really adequately housed there.

They also got rid of Bank Street which was a fairly - very ancient workers' cottages with very few facilities - a pretty rat-infested area down there. I don't think there was any opposition to the new housing. I think people realised there was a crisis, no building had been done and there were a lot of people away overseas in the forces. I think there was a general feeling that, yes, they ought to be housed, and the thing in those days outside toilets were still quite common, central heating and gas stoves were not automatically there, and these houses, although today they would now seem fairly basic, had some new features in them, bathrooms and things like that, being on main drainage, which was a tremendous advantage. I think he was proud of that, because, across the country, I think Cranbrook was one of the leading RDCs in terms of getting to grips with the problem of social housing, and as it developed they were able to build some of the houses on an estate - on an extension of an estate - for resale to their tenants who were sufficiently well off and wanted to own their own houses. They had a scheme absolutely beautifully worked out whereby with the money from the sale of the houses they bought the next tranche of land somewhere, so that when we were reorganised in 1974, the new Borough Council inherited quite a lot of land in and around the settlements, this sort of land bank had been built up by the RDC. Unfortunately the Borough Council squandered most of it on hare-brained schemes or politically correct schemes, but that's another story.

Inevitably he was interested in education although he had so little himself, so he was on the governing bodies of all the local schools, including Cranbrook School and Mary Sheafe, Swattenden, Angley, the Primary School. And I think other primary schools when he became a County Councillor

Bill Jempson's attitude to local party politics and to changes during his time are remembered by his son, Peter..

He was by far the longest serving Chairman of the RDC. He did 47 years on the Parish Council, 45 on the RDC and the Borough Council, and I think he did 16 years in two stints on the County Council. All as an Independent; he never sacrificed his independence, even when local politics were going party. I think a lot of people respected him for being independent. By the time, in particular, when we joined up with Tunbridge Wells Borough in '74, I think he had forgotten more about local government by that stage than most of them would ever learn. They respected his judgement and experience, and I think he had something he knew was right and was worth fighting for. I think people listened to him. I mean, they made him Mayor of the new Borough of Tunbridge Wells in 1978. He took that in his stride. He had been Chairman of the RDC doing much the same sort of thing, entertaining foreign visitors who came to look at Cranbrook's housing or whatever, and going to talk to ministers in London, so I don't think he was overawed. He'd been used to meeting people in one job or another all his life, so they all came alike to him.

The abolition of RDCs and the reorganisation so that we came under Tunbridge Wells was not what he wanted, He was hoping they would merge Cranbrook RD with Tenterden RD so that we would have a homogeneous rural district or borough, but the powers that be... when they do these reorganisations of local government, it's all done by headcount, on population, so in the end they said that Tenterden had to go in with Ashford and we had to go in with Tunbridge Wells, along with bits of Tonbridge Rural, places like Speldhurst and Bidborough. So it wasn't what he wanted. He feared it would be harder for Cranbrook's voice to be heard in the new system, but he was determined that we weren't going to be overawed; you know, historically we go back further than Tunbridge Wells, but quite clearly the urban agglomeration of Southborough/Tunbridge Wells sitting at one end of the borough was always going to produce members and form a larger constituency than the parishes around Cranbrook. But I think he laid the foundations of the idea that Cranbrook was important, and should have its fair share of what money was going.

One of the first things when I took over the seat when he died, I got choked off by two senior town Tory members for saying something they thought of as starting off the old row between town and country. So they had obviously had some of that from my father...

He had a pretty good grasp of detail. A number of times on the Parish Council, the question of who owned a particular strip of land, or whatever, he'd say, " Well, that's County Highways, so get on to so-and-so, or I'll get on to so-and-so at County Hall." Yes, he was tremendously knowledgeable... It helped the people who consulted him. He never had 'surgeries'. It raised a laugh when somebody over in the Borough Council talked about having weekly surgeries or something. I mean, his way, and everybody knew it, was to put on his wellingtons, call in at the post office on his way round to the allotment... and chances are he would get very little gardening time in. People were used to seeing him in his old gardening clothes and wellies and they consulted him. Everybody knew him and where he lived, so, if they had a problem, they decided they needed a haircut or dropped in on him of an evening or they'd ring him up or they'd flag him down when he was in town.

This continued right to the end of his life. He died in January 1991; he wasn't on the County, he'd retired from that, but he was still an active parish and borough councillor. The family bet was that he was spending so much time at meetings that he would actually keel over in a council meeting ..., He didn't quite manage that, but he'd been to meetings up to a fortnight or so before he died.

INDEX OF CONTRIBUTORS

Apps, Geoff.	44, 53.
Barham, Sidney	17, 34, 44, 57, 65, 72.
Blanch, Garry	10, 100.
Brew, Brian	15, 30.
Calcutt, Bill	24, 34.
Camburn, Monica	76, 78.
Dann, Maria	95.
Dann, Nellie	29.
Dann, Rodney	9, 50, 69, 76.
Dapson, Doris	12, 55.
Duxbury, Pat	9, 51, 68.
East, Tom	39.
Enfield, Major	21, 33, 55, 60, 67.
Evernden, Charles	16, 30, 34, 45, 80, 85.
Forward, Charles	8, 15, 27, 38, 81.
Hall, Sonny	16, 100.
Hooper, Dr John	82.
Jempson, Peter	13, 63, 74, 104.
King, Bill	19.
Longley, Brigid	16, 20, 54, 71, 81.
Metson, Nick	8, 47.
Pittock, Mona	70, 75, 77.
Ratcliff, Ted	11, 88.
Rivers, Doreen	92.
Russell, Daphne	64.
Ryan, Edward	11, 48.
Wickham, David	42.
Wickham, John	22.
Woodcock, Eileen	92.

Apology

We are sorry that we have not been able to include interviews with a number of contributors. We would like to thank them for agreeing to take part and to assure them that the tapes and transcripts of all interviews are retained in the Cranbrook Museum archives for future research purposes.

Editorial Team

The publication group was chaired by Betty Carman, who also searched out the photographs.
Interviews were carried out by Betty Carman, Valerie Allen, Brigid Longley, Peter Allen, Tony Allison Janet Attwood and Brian Brew.
Peter Allen and Tony Allison selected the extracts for inclusion in this volume and organised the text.
Brian Brent and Brian Brew converted it into copy for the printers.

The editorial team would particularly like to thank Benita Plows for her invaluable advice on design and preparation of the book for the printers.